POP
MUSIC

CHART-TOPPERS THROUGHOUT HISTORY

THE MUSIC LIBRARY

By Nicole Horning

Portions of this book originally appeared in
The History of American Pop by Stuart A. Kallen.

LUCENT PRESS

Published in 2019 by
Lucent Press, an Imprint of Greenhaven Publishing, LLC
353 3rd Avenue
Suite 255
New York, NY 10010

Copyright © 2019 Greenhaven Press, a part of Gale, Cengage Learning
Gale and Greenhaven Press are registered trademarks used herein under license.

All new materials copyright © 2019 Lucent Press, an Imprint of Greenhaven Publishing, LLC.

All rights reserved. No part of this book may be reproduced in any form without permission in writing from the publisher, except by a reviewer.

Designer: Deanna Paternostro
Editor: Jennifer Lombardo

Library of Congress Cataloging-in-Publication Data

Names: Horning, Nicole, author.
Title: Pop music : chart-toppers throughout history / Nicole Horning.
Description: New York : Lucent Press, [2019] | Series: The music library |
  Includes bibliographical references and index.
Identifiers: LCCN 2018020136 (print) | LCCN 2018022419 (ebook) | ISBN
  9781534565418 (eBook) | ISBN 9781534565401 (library bound book) | ISBN
  9781534565395 (pbk. book)
Subjects: LCSH: Popular music–History and criticism.
Classification: LCC ML3470 (ebook) | LCC ML3470 .H69 2019 (print) | DDC
  781.6409–dc23
LC record available at https://lccn.loc.gov/2018020136

Printed in the United States of America

CPSIA compliance information: Batch #BW19KL: For further information contact Greenhaven Publishing LLC, New York, New York at 1-844-317-7404.

Please visit our website, www.greenhavenpublishing.com. For a free color catalog of all our high-quality books, call toll free 1-844-317-7404 or fax 1-844-317-7405.

Table of Contents

Foreword — 4

Introduction — 6
Pop Music Through the Ages

Chapter One — 11
"All Shook Up": Early Pop Music

Chapter Two — 29
Surfing Songs and Strawberry Fields

Chapter Three — 48
The Rise of Pop Icons

Chapter Four — 64
Tearin' Up Fans' Hearts: Teen Pop of the 1990s

Chapter Five — 78
An Ever-Changing Art Form

Notes — 92

Essential Albums — 96

For More Information — 97

Index — 99

Picture Credits — 103

About the Author — 104

Foreword

Music has a unique ability to speak to people on a deeply personal level and to bring people together. Whether it is experienced through playing a favorite song on a smartphone or at a live concert surrounded by thousands of screaming fans, music creates a powerful connection that sends songs to the top of the charts and artists to the heights of fame.

Music history traces the evolution of those songs and artists. Each generation of musicians builds on the one that came before, and a strong understanding of the artists of the past can help inspire the musical superstars of the future to continue to push boundaries and break new ground.

A closer look at the history of a musical genre also reveals its impact on culture and world events. Music has inspired social change and ignited cultural revolutions. It does more than simply reflect the world; it helps to shape the world.

Music is often considered a universal language. A great song or album speaks to people regardless of age, race, economic status, or nationality. Music from various artists, genres, countries, and time periods might seem completely different at first, but certain themes can be found in all kinds of music: love and loss, success and failure, and life and death. In discovering these similarities, music fans are able to see how many things we all have in common.

Each style of music has its own story, and those stories are filled with colorful characters, shocking events, and songs with true staying power. The Music Library presents those stories to readers with the help of those who know the stories best—music critics, historians, and artists. Annotated quotes by these experts give readers an inside look at a wide variety of musical styles—from early hip-hop and classic country to today's chart-topping pop hits and indie rock favorites. Readers with a passion for music—whether they are headbangers or lovers of

POP MUSIC: CHART-TOPPERS THROUGHOUT HISTORY

Latin music—will discover fun facts about their favorite artists and gain a deeper appreciation for how those artists were influenced by the ones who paved the way in the past.

The Music Library is also designed to serve as an accessible introduction to unfamiliar genres. Suggestions for additional books and websites to explore for more information inspire readers to dive even further into the topics, and the essential albums in each genre are compiled for superfans and new listeners to enjoy. Photographs of some of music's biggest names of the past and present fill the pages, placing readers in the middle of music history.

All music tells a story. Those stories connect people from different places, cultures, and time periods. In understanding the history of the stories told through music, readers discover an exciting way of looking at the past and develop a deeper appreciation for different voices.

INTRODUCTION

Pop Music
Through the Ages

According to *Encyclopaedia Britannica*, pop music is "any commercially oriented music principally intended to be received and appreciated by a wide audience."[1] "Pop music" originally described any music that was popular; however, over time, it has grown into its own genre. As the website Culture Trip stated, "Some believe the pop music genre to be shallow, with simple songs about nothing more than partying, drinking, and sex. But the genre has always been so much more—it's the melting pot of music, a place where sounds of all sorts have been blended together, connected by the melody and structure of traditional pop."[2] Throughout the years, pop music has evolved from songs with country elements in them—such as the songs that Elvis Presley sang—to songs that continue to break boundaries and incorporate new, electronic elements, such as the music of Justin Timberlake.

While some judge pop music to be shallow, it actually covers many deep topics. In fact, pop artists who fail to address important issues are often criticized for it. For instance, in 2018, Justin Timberlake experienced backlash for his *Man of the Woods* album because he did not acknowledge race-related struggles on the album, in interviews, or on social media. In contrast, Kesha created the powerful song "Praying" after allegedly being sexually abused by her former producer, Dr. Luke. She dedicated the song to survivors of sexual assault and to the #MeToo movement, which is a movement that demonstrates how widespread sexual assault and harassment is. Kesha demonstrates the importance of pop music—it defines eras, provides an escape, and offers lyrics that listeners deeply relate to, proving that it is not just shallow, fun music.

Kesha gave an emotional performance of her song "Praying" at the 2018 Grammy Awards, shown here.

Defining the Genre

The pop music genre began in earnest in the era of early rock and roll in the 1950s with artists such as Elvis Presley and producers such as Mitch Miller. Miller defined the pop music genre with his work at Columbia Records. As Columbia's Artists and Repertoire (A&R) director for the pop music division, he selected artists, found songs, suggested musical arrangements, conducted orchestras, and supervised the recording of the songs. Miller had unconventional ideas about music, which led to a pop music boom. Within seven years at Columbia, stores sold around 80 million records that Miller's production work was behind. At one point, eight out of ten songs on the Billboard charts were songs he produced. He said, "I know what I want in a song … A good number has to have self-identification. People want to think: 'This could be me. If I could write words or music to express myself, this is how I'd say it.'"[3] Miller's successful work in the genre opened a path for artists of the 1960s, 1970s, and beyond.

One artist Miller decided not to sign in 1955 was Elvis Presley due to Elvis's manager asking for a five-figure advance and a buyout of his current contract with Sun Records. Elvis began his wildly successful singing career in 1954,

POP MUSIC THROUGH THE AGES | 7

From the very beginning of the pop music genre, pop stars have been adored by fans, who often wait in crowds for hours just to catch a glimpse of their favorite musicians.

becoming internationally popular by 1956. Elvis had a unique sound that combined his numerous musical influences and challenged social norms. With Elvis's success in the 1950s, he brought in a new era of popular music and even starred in movies. While Elvis's popularity continued to climb throughout the early 1960s, another group was quickly rising to fame in Europe, creating a phenomenon that led British reporters to coin a new word to describe it: Beatlemania.

Band Hysteria

The Beatles gained popularity in Europe in early 1963 and the United States in late 1963. The frenzy surrounding the band was something completely new. Even many years after the Beatles' rise and fall, artists' popularity will be compared to Beatlemania, but nothing comes close to the hysteria that surrounded the band. Charles Manson, a criminal and cult leader in the 1960s, even became obsessed with the Beatles and said their music held a secret message that a race war was starting, leading him to order multiple followers of his cult to murder people.

The Beatles are one of the most influential bands across multiple genres, decades, and geographical locations. Even in 2017, former Beatle Paul McCartney still has the power to sell out shows on his tours in just a few minutes. The popularity of the band opened the door for other harmonizing bands to form, such as the Jackson 5, who formed in 1965. While the Jackson 5 created many memorable hits, the most influential and iconic person to come out of the group was Michael Jackson. Even though Michael Jackson sold large numbers of records like the Beatles, there was not the same hysteria among fans of Jackson as there was among Beatles fans. Another focus of fan hysteria was the New Kids on the Block in the 1980s, followed by another boy band craze in the 1990s. Formed in 1993, the Backstreet Boys were a major part of the 1990s boy band craze and are still popular and touring as of 2018. Also formed in the 1990s, *NSYNC was a hugely successful boy band that also led to the successful solo career of one of its members: Justin Timberlake. While the boy band craze seemed to peak in the 1990s, the 2000s also saw the rise and fall of boy bands such as the Jonas Brothers and One Direction.

The 1990s had a boy band craze, but female pop stars of this time were just as popular among fans and were also breaking records. At that time, the Spice Girls were the most successful British group to hit North America since the Beatles. In addition, "they were also the most successful female-pop group, and one of the most successful pop-groups ever, with their single 'Spice Up Your Life.'"[4] As successful as the Spice Girls were, however, their fame was short-lived. They became popular in the United States in 1997, and only four years later, the band officially broke up. While the Spice Girls rose to fame and fell quickly, 1990s stars Britney Spears and Christina Aguilera had huge fan

Even in 2018, the Spice Girls remain one of the best-selling girl groups of all time.

bases and are still performing as of 2018. Christina Aguilera has even been a judge on the singing talent competition television show *The Voice*, helping to find new pop music talent to dominate the charts.

CHAPTER ONE

"All Shook Up": Early Pop Music

Early pop music had a very different sound than pop music does today. When someone thinks of pop music today, they may think of Lady Gaga, Justin Timberlake, or Beyoncé. Clearing the path for these popular musicians today were artists such as Elvis, Bill Haley and His Comets, and Buddy Holly. In addition, Tin Pan Alley was not just a location, but a genre of pop music that arose in the late 1800s, comprising some of the elements of pop music today—ballads and dance music. Even though the music of this era sounds extremely dated compared to modern music, it is still an artist telling their story, expressing themselves through lyrics, and making history. Tin Pan Alley not only paved the way for pop music artists of today, it also introduced musicals with famous Broadway composers such as George Gershwin, Irving Berlin, and Oscar Hammerstein II.

The Beginning of Music Publishing

There was no better place to hear the early musical expressions of minority and immigrant groups than New York City. From 1890 to 1910, between 5,000 and 10,000 European immigrants passed through the federal immigration center on Ellis Island in New York Harbor each day. About 2.5 million of these immigrants were Jews fleeing violent anti-Semitism in Poland, Russia, and other eastern European nations. A large number of them settled in New York City, making it the most populous Jewish community in the world at the time. Some of the most famous singers, songwriters, and performers of the early 20th century had roots in New York's crowded, poverty-stricken Jewish neighborhoods.

As the most populous city in the United States at the time,

New York City was the nation's entertainment capital, and its theaters were legendary. The city was also the business center for theatrical booking, music publishing, recording, and, after 1922, radio broadcasting. The heart of New York's music industry was a short stretch of West 28th Street between Broadway and Sixth Avenue. The street was densely packed

Irving Berlin became an overnight success in 1911, and numerous songs he wrote sold millions of copies.

with old office buildings filled with composers trying to write hit songs on cheap upright pianos. The clattering sound of the pianos playing all at once sounded like pots and pans banging together and gave the street its nickname: Tin Pan Alley.

Tin Pan Alley was home to professional composers who wrote some of the earliest and most influential pop music. They produced hundreds of songs such as "In the Good Old Summertime," "Give My Regards to Broadway," and "Shine on Harvest Moon." These songs were known as standards because they were familiar to everyone and part of the standard repertoire for musicians across the country.

Several of Tin Pan Alley's most admired tunesmiths were the sons of poor Jewish immigrants. Composer and lyricist Irving Berlin was born Israel Baline in Mogilyov, Russia (now called Belarus), in 1888 and grew up on New York's Lower East Side after his family settled there in 1893. Berlin began his career as a singing waiter and began writing song lyrics. His first song, "Marie from Sunny Italy," was published in 1907, and this song is what made him change his name to Irving Berlin. A printer's error listed his name as Irving Berlin instead of Israel Baline on the song, and he decided to keep it. Berlin found overnight success in 1911 by writing "Alexander's Ragtime Band." The sheet music of the song sold 1.5 million copies in the first 18 months after its release—it was even played on the *Titanic* as it began to sink. The recording of the song by singer Arthur Collins was the best-selling record for 10 weeks, and "Alexander's Ragtime Band" was recorded in later years by hundreds of popular artists.

In the 60 years that followed his first hit, Berlin went on to write dozens of legendary songs, including "Blue Skies," "There's No Business Like Show Business," and "God Bless America." Berlin's "White Christmas," first recorded by singer Bing Crosby in 1942, is one of the best-selling records of all time, with sales of more than 50 million. Later recordings of "White Christmas" by other artists sold an additional 120 million records.

There were many other classics written by Jewish American composers during the golden age of Tin Pan Alley that dated from the 1920s to the 1930s. These hits included Irving Caesar's "Tea For Two" and "Swanee," George Gershwin's "I Got Rhythm," and Jack Yellen's "Ain't She Sweet" and "Happy Days Are Here Again."

While the songs of Tin Pan Alley may sound old-fashioned to modern ears, they

HITS DETERMINED BY PAPER

Today, a music hit is often determined by what position it is in on the Billboard charts and how long it stays there. However, in the 1800s and early 1900s, there were no Billboard charts to gauge how popular a song or artist was, and the number of sales of records did not determine popularity, either. A song was determined to be a hit based on how many copies of the song's sheet music were sold. During the 1800s, pianos were a primary source of entertainment in the home, and therefore, sheet music was in high demand. With a piano and sheet music, families could play the hits of the day in their home. Generally, "sheet music consisted of four or five pages of musical notation scored for voice and piano (and sometimes even ukulele) and wrapped in attractive covers."[1] Sheet music was a profitable product for this era—millions of copies were sold by 1910, and composers and performers worked hard to produce music to meet the demand for sheet music. However, once phonograph recordings became popular, sheet music sales declined.

During the Tin Pan Alley era, a hit song was determined by how many copies of sheet music, such as the piece shown here, were sold.

1. Bob Batchelor, *American Pop: Popular Culture Decade by Decade*. Westport, CT: Greenwood Press, 2009, p. 315.

POP MUSIC: CHART-TOPPERS THROUGHOUT HISTORY

established rules for pop music that continue to influence songwriters. Tin Pan Alley composers used specific song themes based on romantic love, heartbreak, patriotism, and home and family. The lyrics were simple and the melodies memorable. Like many pop songs of later decades, Tin Pan Alley hits had 16 measures, or bars, for each verse. Almost every song starts with a brief instrumental introduction, called a hook, that helps listeners instantly identify the song. A verse is sung that explains the subject matter of the song. This is followed by a refrain, or chorus, that is repeated after every verse.

Most Tin Pan Alley songs—and most pop songs today—have three verse-chorus sections. Some have an extra part called a bridge after the second chorus. The bridge has a different melody and rhythm than the rest of the song and provides a contrast to the repetitive verse-chorus pattern.

"Over the Rainbow"

During the height of Tin Pan Alley, the sales of sheet music determined the popularity of a song and whether it was a hit. However, technological advances in the 1920s in radio and film created a unified popular culture for the first time, and a hit was determined by more than just sheet music.

Radio experienced the fastest growth of any new medium. By 1922, there were 564 radio stations in the United States. Within five years, national broadcasters such as NBC and CBS carried live broadcasts of popular singers and dance bands and also played records. This allowed listeners across the United States to hear the same music. This development brought millions of dollars to the entertainment industry and laid the foundation for the record business as it is known today.

Pop music got another boost in 1927 when the first movies with sound were produced. In the decades that followed, movies were a prime driver of pop music trends. For example, in 1939, actress Judy Garland sang the song "Over the Rainbow" in the film *The Wizard of Oz*. The song became a pop hit and helped make Garland a musical star. The song is considered by many to be the best movie song in history, but it almost did not make the final film because the production company thought it slowed down the opening Kansas sequence of the movie. They were proven wrong when "Over the Rainbow" went on to win an Academy Award for Best Song and was re-recorded numerous times. *TIME* magazine included it in its list of "All-Time 100 Songs," stating, "The tune itself is pop perfection. At

"Over the Rainbow" was recorded for The Wizard of Oz in 1939 and is still an iconic pop song in 2018. Judy Garland is shown here singing the song in the movie.

just over two minutes, its lilting, free-floating melody and uplifting orchestral backing perfectly evoke Dorothy's hopes of leaving the only home she's known. The song has been covered countless times, and for years, the original movie version wasn't even the most popular one."[5]

The powerful pop song has provided comfort for numerous people since its first recording in 1939. During World War II, a special recording of the song by Judy Garland with the Tommy Dorsey Orchestra was sent out to soldiers to give them hope, and Garland also performed the song live for the soldiers in 1943. Later, the song became an anthem for the LGBT+ community. According to the BBC, "the 'rainbow' in the lyrics [matched] the multicoloured flag of inclusion flown at Pride marches, and the term 'friend of Dorothy' even [became] a knowing reference for gay men. Her frail and trembling voice embodied both the fragility of hope in dark times, and the yearning that something good will eventually happen."[6]

The song has been covered by country music artist Willie Nelson, Rufus Wainwright, and the cast of the television show *Glee*. "Over the Rainbow" has even been used by the National Aeronautics and Space Administration (NASA) to awaken astronauts in the morning. The song provided particular comfort after the shooting at Sandy Hook Elementary in Newtown, Connecticut, when the elementary school's choir recorded it. One of the most popular recordings of the song was by Israel Kamakawiwoʻole, who sang the song while playing a ukulele. At the One Love Manchester benefit concert in 2017, which occurred two weeks after a bomb attack at an Ariana Grande concert in Manchester, England, Grande sang a very emotional version of the song to offer consolation and hope to those watching.

Developments in the Music Industry

"Over the Rainbow" was a hit by all accounts, and around this time, the music industry trade magazine *Billboard* began tracking hit songs and records. In 1936, the magazine issued three Top 10 charts from three record companies. In 1940, it created a unified chart, an early version of the hit parade. This chart was created by tracking what was selling well in 50 stores. In this era, before rock and roll, pop music was dominated by slow, romantic ballads. Musical arrangements featured syrupy violins, swirling woodwinds, and pianos. Drums were not played on these records—the weak rhythms were kept by the soft thump of the stand-up bass.

Early 1950s hit parade songs were often recycled from earlier decades. The song "Yellow Rose of Texas" by orchestra leader Mitch Miller was composed in the 1850s. Singer Eddie Fisher's "Oh My Papa" was a song from an older stage musical. Other big sellers were silly novelty songs such as "How Much is that Doggie in the Window?" and "If I Knew You Were Comin' (I'd've Baked a Cake)."

One of the few interesting developments in the music industry at this time was a new type of vinyl record that replaced poor-quality 78 revolutions per minute (RPM) records, which held about

RECORD CHANGES

New technology in radio and records drove popular music sales in the first half of the 20th century. The record revolution began in June 1948 when Ed Wallerstein, chairman of Columbia Records, held a press conference at the prestigious Waldorf Astoria Hotel in New York City. Wallerstein directed the reporters' attention to a stack of 78 RPM records on one side of the stage and a pile of 33⅓ RPM records on other side. Wallerstein gestured dramatically at the smaller pile and pointed out that the 33⅓ RPM, or LP records, held as much music as the towering pile of old-fashioned 78 records. In addition, the 33⅓ records were made from a relatively new material, vinyl plastic, which was virtually indestructible.

Shown here is an example of a 45 RPM single. Listeners could flip it over to hear the song "Shut Down" on the B side.

Vinyl records had a much better sound than 78 records, which contained cracks, clicks, and scratches that were often louder than the music. The new records were also available in stereo, with right and left channels that allowed instruments and voices to be separated on the recording. Perhaps the most revolutionary change in records in the late 1940s was the introduction of the 45 RPM single. Most pop singles in the following decades had one song on the "A side" that was chosen as a possible hit, while the flip side, or "B side," held a song by the same artist that was considered less commercial.

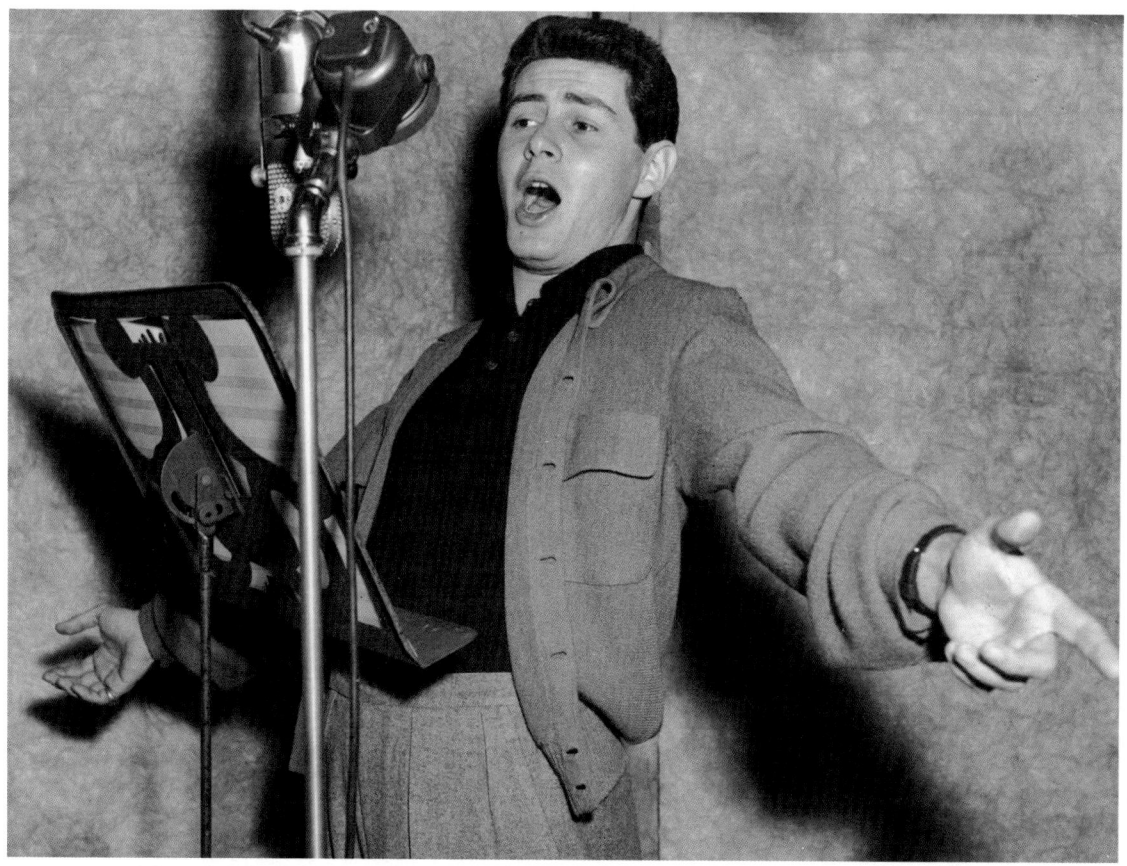

Eddie Fisher began singing at the age of 12. One of his most famous songs was "Oh My Papa," which was actually composed in the 1930s.

3 minutes of music per side. The new records had a higher quality sound and were unbreakable. Singles, which played at 45 RPM, held one 3- to 4-minute song on each side. Long-playing (LP) records, which played at 33⅓ RPM, could be up to 30 minutes in length and hold around 6 songs on each side.

"Rock Around the Clock"

In 1945, after the end of World War II, veterans returned home, married, and started families. Called the baby boom, this time period lasted about 20 years, and during this period, more than 76 million babies were born in the United States. By 1958, there were 19 million teenagers in America, and by the mid-1960s, more than 40 percent of all Americans were under the age of 20. Throughout the 1950s, baby boomers developed their own teen culture, which was spread to every village, town, and city by popular music.

"ALL SHOOK UP": EARLY POP MUSIC

If American teenagers liked a song, they went out and bought it with their allowances. This could make any song a best-selling pop phenomenon overnight. No one understood this better than Bill Haley, who started his career in the 1940s as the "Rambling Yodeler" in a country-and-western band called the Saddlemen. Like many country singers, Haley loved the blues and boogie-woogie music. In 1952, the Saddlemen changed their band's name to Bill Haley and His Comets to record the song "Crazy, Man, Crazy."

Haley based the song's title and lyrics on teenage slang he heard when his band played at high school dances. Musically, "Crazy, Man, Crazy" combines a boogie-woogie bass beat with a honky-tonk guitar sound, all played in a 12-bar blues format. This hybrid of music styles came to define rock-and-roll music throughout the 1950s. It also propelled "Crazy, Man, Crazy" to number 12 on the Billboard chart, making it the first rock-and-roll song to become a pop hit. When "Crazy, Man, Crazy" was used on the "Glory in the Flower" episode of the CBS television show *Omnibus*, it was the first rock song ever played on TV.

Haley's biggest success, "(We're Gonna) Rock Around the Clock" (now known simply as "Rock Around the Clock"), became a rock-and-roll anthem in 1955. Ironically, the lyrics were not written by a boogie-woogie bluesman, but by a 63-year-old music industry veteran, Max Freedman.

When Haley initially recorded "Rock Around the Clock" in 1954, it was a moderate hit. One year later, however, when the song blasted out loudly over the opening credits of the film *Blackboard Jungle*, it caused a sensation. *Blackboard Jungle* was about a group of rebellious teenagers in an inner-city school who smash their teacher's prized collection of 78 RPM jazz records. In several cities throughout the United States and Europe, the movie brought out rowdy mobs of teenagers who frightened adults by singing, pounding on seats, and throwing popcorn. There were even minor riots in several cities. "Rock Around the Clock" was re-released and quickly sold 6 million copies, making it the best-selling record in history at that time. Music journalist Fred Bronson explained that the song was more than just a hit: "It was a signal flare, warning that all that followed would be different from all that came before."[7]

Discovering Elvis

Haley's music might have been a warning signal, but no one was prepared for the musical explosion that was catching fire in Memphis,

Tennessee. Located north of the Delta on the Mississippi River, Memphis was at the crossroads of musical culture in the early 1950s. Blues players from the Delta and jazz bands from New Orleans, Louisiana, played the nightclubs that catered to an African American clientele on the city's famed Beale Street.

Memphis also attracted white musicians from across the South. Some cut records at Sun Studios, a recording studio and the home of the Sun Records recording label, founded by recording engineer Sam Phillips and his assistant Marion Keisker. In the early 1950s, Phillips struggled to earn a living making records by Delta guitar wizards such as B. B. King and Howlin' Wolf, who went on to become blues legends in later years. To make ends meet, Sun allowed amateur musicians into the studios to make records for their families and friends. One such customer, a poor 18-year-old truck driver named Elvis Presley from Tupelo, Mississippi, entered the studio with his guitar in July 1953. He paid Keisker around $4 to record a personal album for his mother.

Phillips paid little attention to Elvis, but Keisker took notice of his unique singing style. Meanwhile, Phillips continued to face

Sam Phillips was looking for a musician who could blend the best of white and black music, and he found that in Elvis Presley.

"ALL SHOOK UP": EARLY POP MUSIC

financial problems because white radio stations would not play the African American music he was recording. Phillips told Keisker he needed to discover a white man who could sing R&B songs to bridge the gap and blend the best of both white and black music: "If I could find a white man with the Negro sound and the Negro feel, I could make a million dollars."[8] Keisker suggested Elvis, and Phillips called him into the studio.

The Rise of an Icon

In a July 1954 recording session, Elvis recorded the blues song "That's All Right (Mama)" by Arthur "Big Boy" Crudup, an African American blues musician. Crudup's 1946 recording featured lyrics that were shouted out over driving drums, a swinging guitar, and a walking bass line. Elvis's version, with studio musicians Scotty Moore on guitar, Bill Black on stand-up bass, and no drums, sounded like a fast-tempo country song.

Elvis also recorded a rocking version of the country waltz "Blue Moon of Kentucky" to back the single. Phillips quickly understood he had found the musician he was looking for. Moore said on one side of the single, "Elvis took a blues song and sang it white," and on the other side of the single, "he took a country song and gave it a bluesy spin."[9]

Much of this musical style had to do with Elvis's voice, described by music professor Richard Middleton as "swooping almost two octaves at times, changing timbre from a croon to a growl instantaneously ... sometimes within the course of a single phrase."[10] "That's All Right (Mama)" became a regional Memphis hit when it was played repeatedly on country-and-western radio stations.

Elvis was at first marketed as "the Hillbilly Cat," but he was not a country-and-western cowboy. With his satin jacket, pompadour hairdo, long sideburns, and pelvis-shaking dance moves, Elvis drove teenage girls wild. The singer's popularity attracted the attention of RCA Records, the biggest record company in America, which bought his contract from Phillips in November 1955. Phillips continued to produce innovative new artists, including country singer Johnny Cash and rockers Roy Orbison and Jerry Lee Lewis.

On January 27, 1956, RCA released Elvis's emotion-charged "Heartbreak Hotel." The next day, Elvis appeared on national television for the first time. He sang "Heartbreak Hotel" on a program called *Stage Show*. On April 3, when Elvis sang the song on *The Milton Berle Show*, an estimated one-quarter of America's teenage

Elvis's dance moves were so controversial that when he made a television appearance, he could only be shown from the waist up.

"ALL SHOOK UP": EARLY POP MUSIC

population was watching. By this time, Billboard's pop music chart was called the Hot 100. "Heartbreak Hotel" was number 1 for 8 weeks and went on to become the best-selling single of 1956. This was Elvis's first gold record, a designation for records that sold more than 500,000 copies.

Elvis quickly became a pop sensation. Girls swooned over his singing, while boys picked up guitars and began styling their hair into pompadours. This created a media backlash. When Elvis appeared on The *Ed Sullivan Show*, he was shown only from the waist up because his dancing was considered inappropriate for television. *TIME* magazine described Elvis's famous dance move as "a frantic quiver, as if he had swallowed a jack-hammer."[11]

By the end of 1956, *Billboard* reported that Elvis had charted more songs than any other artist in the history of the magazine. Combined sales of his singles "Hound Dog," "Don't Be Cruel," "Jailhouse Rock," "All Shook Up," and "Love Me Tender" reached 50,000 copies a day. Many of these early singles were backed by the strong, driving rhythm of drummer J. D. Fontana, while Bill Black slapped the strings of his stand-up bass. This sound came to be known as rockabilly, or rock and roll performed by hillbilly musicians.

From Hits to Heartbreak

Elvis was adored by fans and quickly became a teen idol. Additionally, not only were fans able to listen to his music and watch his television performances, but they were also able to see him in movies—Elvis acted in more than 30 movies over an eight-year span. With time, there was not as much controversy over him and his performances. He became a predictable entertainer. In addition, there were many changes in the music world in the 1960s—mainly the rise of the Beatles and the Rolling Stones.

By the late 1960s, Elvis was still an icon, but he was not as much of a teen idol anymore and hit songs were more rare. Unfortunately, as his fame started to dwindle, he also took on a lethal lifestyle that involved unhealthy eating and an addiction to prescription pills. In the mid-1970s, his career came to a standstill—he did not record much music and barely performed concerts. On August 16, 1977, Elvis died. Fans across the world mourned the death of such an important figure in multiple genres of music. Many of these fans gathered at his home, Graceland, in Memphis. Even today, fans still mourn the death of the teen idol and music icon, and his albums and other Elvis merchandise continue to sell. However, some still do not believe that he is dead, and there

This photo, taken at Graceland two days before the 20th anniversary of Elvis's death, shows how much love his fans still have for him.

are plenty of conspiracy theories that his death was faked. Some claim to have seen him at a Burger King in Kalamazoo, Michigan. Other conspiracy theories suggest he is a reptilian shapeshifter or was an extra in the movie *Home Alone*. There is also a theory that he is a groundskeeper at Graceland, which is still a top tourist attraction in the United States, especially around the times of Elvis's birthday and death date. Fans even have the opportunity to stay in the guest house.

The Talent and Scandal of Jerry Lee Lewis

In a 1986 interview, Phillips said, "Elvis had a certain type of total charisma that was just almost untouchable by any other human that I know of or have ever seen."[12] Phillips also noted the piano-pounding Jerry Lee Lewis was the most talented person he ever worked with.

Lewis's 1957 singles "Whole Lotta Shakin' Goin' On" and "Great Balls of Fire" went straight to the top of Billboard's country-and-western and R&B charts. "Whole Lotta Shakin'

"ALL SHOOK UP": EARLY POP MUSIC

Goin' On" hit number 3 on the pop charts. His antics onstage and off earned him the nickname "Killer." When Lewis performed, he climbed on top of his piano to sing or pounded the keys with his feet. There is also a story that on one occasion, he lit an expensive, handcrafted piano on fire. Lewis sometimes confirms and sometimes denies this story. However, J. W. Brown, Lewis's bass player around this time, says it never happened.

While Lewis set the tone for wild rock-and-roll performers for years to come, his career was short-lived. In 1958, as he was stepping off a plane in Europe with his 13-year-old cousin Myra Brown, he told the British press that she was his wife. The news quickly spread to the United States, and although he continued to make music, the scandal derailed Lewis's career, and he never again reached the level of stardom he had when he first recorded for Sun Studios.

Buddy Holly

Buddy Holly, from Lubbock, Texas, helped make the electric Fender Stratocaster guitar famous and shaped how music is played today. Holly's guitar gave a bright, sharp sound to his late-1950s rockabilly hits such as "That'll Be the Day," "Rave On," "Oh Boy," and "Peggy Sue." When Holly appeared on the scene with his distinctive eyeglasses and his Stratocaster hanging around his neck, he became an instant rock icon. Holly's songs have been covered by dozens of pop artists since the late 1950s and have come to define the rockabilly era of pop music.

Buddy Holly's career was cut tragically short. On February 3, 1959, he was killed in a small plane crash in Iowa along with pop star

RIAA

In 1958, the Recording Industry Association of America (RIAA) started tracking album and song sales and giving them an award based on the number of sales. For a song to be certified gold, it has to sell 500,000 units, and for a platinum certification, it is 1 million units. For a song to be certified multi-platinum, it has to sell 2 million units.

The album certification levels work the same way as the songs. For an album to be certified gold, it has to sell 500,000 units; this tier was established in 1958. For an album to be certified platinum, it has to sell 1 million units, and this tier was established in 1976. The multi-platinum award was established in 1984 and means an album sold at least 2 million units. In 1999, the diamond award was created for album sales of more than 10 million.

Ritchie Valens and novelty songwriter J. P. "the Big Bopper" Richardson. This marked the end of the initial phase of rock and roll, which lasted a little more than five years. Commenting on this era, *Rolling Stone* magazine's music critic Robert Palmer wrote, "Rock & roll's takeover of the pop-music marketplace in the mid-fifties was as threatening to the entrenched old-line music and entertainment business as it was to professional authority figures everywhere."[13]

By 1960, old-line pop producers were sanitizing rock and roll, promoting teen idols such as Frankie Avalon, Paul Anka, and Bobby Darin, who did not shout or growl out the lyrics but crooned them sweetly. Commenting on this phenomenon, notable Cleveland, Ohio, disc jockey Bill Randle said in *Billboard*'s December 1958 issue, "I think tastes have changed … Rock and roll is being integrated into

Buddy Holly (center) popularized the electric Fender Stratocaster guitar, changing how music was played from then on.

"ALL SHOOK UP": EARLY POP MUSIC

popular music. It's no longer a novelty. Rock and roll was an earthy, virile influence, but the authentic artists were destroyed."[14]

The End of an Era

By the late 1950s, the icons that had dominated the era had disappeared—Buddy Holly's life and career were tragically cut short, Jerry Lee Lewis's career was never the same after the marriage to his young cousin was spread throughout the press, and Elvis's army service from 1958 to 1960 took him out of the music business shortly after he entered it. When Elvis came back, he was not seen as controversial anymore, he started making movies, and his hit songs eventually were few and far between. With the end of this first phase of pop music with a rock and roll influence, new pop bands that were influenced by these groundbreaking musicians emerged. The emergence of these bands would forever change the music scene, and they would become icons themselves.

CHAPTER TWO

Surfing Songs
and Strawberry Fields

Some of the most influential bands in pop music started in the 1960s. Additionally, the bands did not all come from one region, which created a mix of unique sounds on the radio. Some, such as the Beatles, eventually stopped making music together, with each member splintering off and creating their own music. Others, such as the Beach Boys, continue to tour and create new music, even though some of the band members have passed away. However, regardless of the status of the band in 2018, there is no doubt in the music world or in fans' minds that some of the best pop stars emerged in the 1960s and are still highly influential.

"Surfin' USA"

In the 1960s, California was idealized in films and on TV shows as a carefree, sun-kissed place where summer never ended. In the world of pop music, no one generated better musical imagery of surf, sand, and sunshine than the Beach Boys. The original group consisted of Brian Wilson, Dennis Wilson, Carl Wilson, Mike Love, and Al Jardine. David Marks and Bruce Johnston joined the band later. Their music consisted largely of positive, upbeat songs that spoke of cars and surfing. These short, fun songs had lyrics such as

If everybody had an ocean across the U.S.A.
then everybody'd be surfin' like California ...

Tell the teacher we're surfin'
Surfin' U.S.A.[15]

Songs such as these were incredibly popular, as was the band itself—the group has had 54 songs on the Billboard Hot 100 chart, 15 top 10 hits, and 4 number 1 hits.

Brothers Brian, Dennis, and Carl Wilson were encouraged to explore and make music by their parents. Their father,

Shown here from left to right are Mike Love, David Marks, Brian Wilson, Dennis Wilson, and Carl Wilson: the members of the Beach Boys. Marks filled in for Al Jardine while he served in the Navy.

Murry, was a songwriter who worked at a machinery shop. As teenagers, the Wilson brothers formed a band with their cousin Mike Love and friends Al Jardine and David Marks. Dennis Wilson had taken up the emerging sport of surfing and convinced the rest of the group to write songs about it. Shortly after forming, the band, with Marks as a replacement for Jardine, had a hit with their song "Surfin'" in 1961. In 1962, they were signed to Capitol Records. Brian Wilson enjoyed composing songs, and he would write nearly all of their songs for years. This format worked—their first album reached number 14 and singles off of the album landed on the Billboard charts. In 1963, soon after signing with Capitol, Jardine reclaimed his place, and the band released its second album, *Surfin' USA*. With their third album, *Surfer Girl*, Brian took over full artistic control. This kind of independence while being signed to a major record label was something that was unheard-of. Brian was able to secure full control of writing, arranging, and producing the Beach Boys' songs.

However, in 1964, Brian decided to withdraw from touring with the band due to drugs and stress-related breakdowns. First, he was replaced by Glen Campbell, then by Bruce Johnston. Even though he was not a visible member of the band on tours, he continued to maintain artistic control over their music. In 1966, one of the band's most famous albums, *Pet Sounds*, was released. In 2016, 50 years after the album's release, Jordan Runtagh of *Rolling Stone* magazine wrote of *Pet Sounds*, "The result was an album that had leading musical figures struggling to match his technical innovation, lyrical depth and melodic genius. Half a century later, it's questionable whether anyone has." In addition, the album "took up more than 10 months and cost a then-unheard-of $70,000, making it one of the most expensive albums ever recorded at that time."[16] *Pet Sounds* also did not have upbeat, fun songs similar to the ones the Beach Boys had produced in the past, such as "Fun, Fun, Fun," "I Get Around," and "Barbara Ann." It was a much more personal, artistic album, and Capitol Records tried to bury it instead of promoting it.

Capitol's Burial of *Pet Sounds*

Pet Sounds is a highly influential album that helped make pop music what it is today. It is a masterpiece album that has been inspirational for numerous musicians from the 1960s to the current day. As a 2016 article in *The Atlantic* stated, "Wilson's bildungsroman [coming-of-age story] about the life and death of adolescent love wasn't just a great record: It was also a record of a great artist's mind—popular music's first long-form investigation into the psyche [mind] of an [artist] … With *Pet Sounds*, Wilson brought an ambition to pop that it hadn't previously known and helped make heroes out of producers."[17]

This influential album did not sit well at a Capitol marketing meeting from the start. Capitol was hoping for an album that would be packed with hits to return on the company's $70,000 investment. However, when the final mix of the album was played at a meeting, executives were horrified by the lack of upbeat sounds that the Beach Boys were famous for producing. Karl Engermann, an executive with Capitol Records at the time, said, "It was played at a sales meeting, and the marketing guys were really disappointed and down about the record, because it wasn't the normal 'Surfin' U.S.A.,' 'Help Me,

Rhonda,' 'Barbara Ann,' kind of production." Beach Boy Bruce Johnston said, "Capitol didn't see the evolution ... *Pet Sounds* was so radical compared to the nice 'Barbara Anns' we had been making, which Capitol had been successfully selling and they just wanted more."[18]

Capitol's answer to *Pet Sounds* was to quickly release a greatest-hits album and throw its entire promotional machine behind that one instead. Runtagh wrote,

> Best of the Beach Boys *was rushed into shops less than two months after* Pet Sounds'

The failure of Capitol Records to promote *Pet Sounds* could have been disastrous for the Beach Boys' career, but fans saw the album's value and bought it anyway.

release. It promptly went gold, while *Pet Sounds, effectively left to sell on its own merits, barely cracked the Top 10. It was a major drop-off from the Number One million-sellers of prior years. Capitol felt vindicated, and Brian Wilson was crushed. "In my heart of hearts, I think that the reason* [Pet Sounds] *isn't a billion-selling album is simply that the label didn't believe in Brian," Johnston reflected [in 1996]. "They turned their back on him by releasing* Best of the Beach Boys. *Why wouldn't you allocate a massive budget to promote* Pet Sounds? *This album is timeless and forever, and the label [ignored it.]"*[19]

Even though Capitol Records ignored *Pet Sounds*, choosing to focus instead on a greatest-hits album that the Beach Boys originally had no intention of releasing, fans saw the value of the album that Capitol did not. The members of the Beatles used it to inspire their own album; without *Pet Sounds*, the famous Beatles album *Sgt. Pepper's Lonely Hearts Club Band* would not exist. Former Beatle Paul McCartney said,

The big influence was Pet Sounds *by The Beach Boys. That was the album that flipped me. The musical invention on that album was, like, "Wow!" That was the big thing for me. I just thought, "Oh dear me. This is the album of all time. What … are we going to do?" So,* Sgt Pepper *eventually came out, basically, from the idea that I had about this band. It was going to be an album of another band that wasn't us.*[20]

Ironically, the Beatles' *Rubber Soul* album is what inspired *Pet Sounds*. After listening to *Rubber Soul*, Brian said, "I have to record an album as good or better than 'Rubber Soul.' If I ever do anything in my life, I'm going to make that good an album."[21] McCartney has also stated that "God Only Knows" off of *Pet Sounds* "is his favorite song in all of music history."[22]

One song that did not make it onto *Pet Sounds* that is also considered a masterpiece is "Good Vibrations." The song was originally supposed to be on the album, but Brian thought it needed more work, and it appeared on the album *Smiley Smile* in 1967. This song took about 80 studio sessions over a seven-month span to complete. Studio musicians would be brought in for sessions that lasted anywhere between 10 minutes and 6 hours for work on just this song. They were sometimes asked to rework a tiny section of the song over and over until it fit with Brian's vision.

SURFING SONGS AND STRAWBERRY FIELDS

The work put into the song was worth it—it was the Beach Boys' third number 1 hit, and Brian's last. After finishing "Good Vibrations," depression and drug use made it hard for him to continue his work, and he went into seclusion.

The Dark Side of Pop Music

After Brian left the band, the Beach Boys did not have the same success. In 1968, Dennis Wilson fell under the spell of then-unknown cult leader Charles Manson, who led a group known as the Manson Family. In the summer of 1968, Dennis Wilson offered a ride to two hitchhiking women, Patricia Krenwinkel and Ella Jo Bailey. On the way, they told him about a musician and spiritual guru they were living with named Charlie, who wanted to meet him. Krenwinkel and Bailey introduced Wilson to Charles Manson, and they quickly hit it off. Soon, the entire Family had moved into Wilson's home.

Manson had dreams of being a musician and played guitar for Wilson while also teaching him how to play it—Wilson was a drummer and therefore had never learned how to play guitar. Later in the summer, Wilson suggested Manson should come into the studio and record his music. He also introduced him to producer Terry Melcher. At first, Melcher showed interest in Manson's music. However, he later changed his mind and did not want to work with Manson. Manson did not take the news well—Wilson was a well-connected musician whom Manson was counting on to get him a recording contract. Manson pulled a knife on Wilson, and he moved out of his own home. However, in the fall of 1968,

> *the Beach Boys recorded a version of Manson's "Cease to Exist," changing some of the lyrics and re-naming it "Never Learn Not to Love." The song, credited to Dennis Wilson as the only writer, later found its way onto a Beach Boys album.*

Not long after, Wilson found a bullet on his bed. "I gave him a bullet," Manson later said, "because he changed the words to my song."[23]

At the time, Wilson did not realize that he had let an extremely dangerous person into his life. Manson had taken courses based on Dale Carnegie's book *How to Win Friends and Influence People*. While the courses were for businesspeople, Manson used these tactics for manipulating people, which he combined with racism. This is how he grew such a following in his cult. In 1969, Manson was still upset that Melcher did not give him a record deal. He wanted revenge as well as to kick-start a race war, so he sent the Family to Melcher's residence. However, he did not know that Melcher had moved out and rented the house to movie director Roman Polanski and his wife, actress Sharon Tate. On the night of August 9, 1969, Manson directed Family members Patricia Krenwinkel, Susan Atkins, and Tex Watson, with Laura Kasabian as lookout, to the Melcher residence to seek his revenge. He told them to murder the people inside and make it look like the Black Panther party (an African American political organization that challenged police brutality in the 1960s) committed the murders. Polanski's pregnant wife, along with Jay Sebring, Voytek Frykowski, Abigail Folger, and Steven Parent were all murdered by the Family. The next night, Manson accompanied Watson, Krenwinkel, Atkins, Kasabian, Leslie Van Houten, and Steve "Clem" Grogan to murder two more randomly chosen victims: Leno and Rosemary LaBianca. Written on the walls at each crime scene were the words "pig" and "Helter Skelter," which was the title of a Beatles song. Although many people were murdered, the incident became known in the press as the Tate-LaBianca murders.

The members of the Family who committed the murders were caught in November and December 1969 after Susan Atkins, who was

Charles Manson (shown here) quickly latched onto Beach Boy Dennis Wilson in the hope of getting a recording contract. However, when Terry Melcher did not give him one, Manson sought revenge within a year.

SURFING SONGS AND STRAWBERRY FIELDS   35

in jail for a different crime, was telling another inmate about the Tate-LaBianca murders. The inmate told the authorities, leading to the arrest of Watson, Manson, Krenwinkel, Kasabian, and Van Houten. Atkins died in prison in 2009; Grogan was released from prison on parole in 1986; Krenwinkel is still in prison as of 2018 after being denied parole in 2017; Van Houten is still in prison as of 2018 and was denied parole in 2018; as of 2018, Watson is still in prison after being denied parole in 2016; Kasabian was not jailed after agreeing to be a key witness in the trials; and Manson died in prison on November 19, 2017. Dennis felt guilt over the Tate-LaBianca murders for the rest of his life because he had introduced Manson to Melcher. He also felt guilt over knowing Manson and the Family before the murders were committed.

This turmoil was not the last to affect the Beach Boys. In 1970, they parted ways with Capitol and signed with Warner Brothers. After *Pet Sounds*, their albums sold modestly, and in 1976, Brian re-emerged with the Beach Boys for *15 Big Ones*. The Beach Boys were

The Beach Boys are still active as a band today. In 2012, they went on a 50th Anniversary Reunion Tour and released a new album.

POP MUSIC: CHART-TOPPERS THROUGHOUT HISTORY

"HELTER SKELTER"

In addition to latching onto Dennis Wilson, Charles Manson also became obsessed with an album from another pop group at the time, even though he had never met them. The self-titled album *The Beatles*, frequently known as the White Album, had songs such as "Blackbird," "Piggies," and "Helter Skelter," which all had different meanings in Charles Manson's mind. He believed the songs foretold a race war. However, when the race war that Manson believed would happen did not occur, he decided he needed to kickstart it with murder, which is why he instructed members of the Family to make it look like the Black Panther party committed the Tate-LaBianca murders—he wanted to pit black and white people against each other. In a 2017 article in *Newsweek*, Linley Sanders wrote of Manson's take on "Helter Skelter,"

> There are no references to race in the song, which actually refers to the British English term "helter skelter" meaning "confused." The song itself has lyrics that refer to an amusement park ride, with Paul McCartney singing, "When I get to the bottom / I go back to the top of the slide / Where I stop and turn / And I go for a ride / Till I get to the bottom and I see you again."
>
> Nonetheless, Manson interpreted the lyrics as a sign that the race war was imminent and that black Americans would first defeat white Americans, but then be unable to run the country without his help.[1]

Manson believed each song on the White Album had a secret message in it just for the Family, directing them toward violent revolution among other things. He also believed he heard secret messages in the Beatles album *The Magical Mystery Tour*.

"Helter Skelter" is one of the most-covered Beatles songs, and some bands, such as U2, have made references to Manson stealing the song from the Beatles and stated that they are reclaiming it by covering it.

The way their music turned into a soundtrack for a murderous cult was deeply distressing for the Beatles. Paul McCartney said, "He interpreted the whole thing ... and arrived at having to go out and kill everyone ... it was frightening, because you don't write songs for those reasons."[2]

1. Linley Sanders, "Charles Manson is Dead: What Was His 'Helter Skelter' Race War Plan?," *Newsweek*, November 20, 2017. www.newsweek.com/charles-manson-what-was-helter-skelter-race-war-plan-716925.

2. Quoted in Kory Grow, "Charles Manson: How Cult Leader's Twisted Beatles Obsession Inspired Family Members," *Rolling Stone*, August 9, 2017. www.rollingstone.com/culture/features/charles-manson-twisted-beatles-obsession-inspired-murders-w459333.

reunited and seemed destined for success again, but then tragedy struck when Dennis drowned in 1983. In 1985, the acclaimed record *The Beach Boys* was released, and in 1988, the Beach Boys released their hit song "Kokomo." The song gave the Beach Boys their first number 1 since "Good Vibrations" and sold more than 1 million singles. The same year it was released, the Beach Boys appeared on an episode of the TV show *Full House* to sing "Kokomo" as well as "Barbara Ann." The Beach Boys were frequent guests on the show because John Stamos, who played Uncle Jesse on the show, had been touring with them often since 1985. While being a guest on a famous TV show was a huge deal, something even bigger happened to them that same year—they were inducted into the Rock & Roll Hall of Fame.

Since then, the band continues to face turmoil. In 1998, Carl Wilson died of lung cancer, and the rest of the surviving founding members continue to face legal issues over the rights to the band's name. However, despite these challenges, the band members still tour and make music. In 2012, Brian, Mike Love, Al Jardine, Bruce Johnston, and David Marks reunited to tour for their 50th anniversary and released a new album called *That's Why God Made the Radio*.

Brill Building Songwriters

There is little doubt that some of the biggest names in 1960s pop were inspired by the first generation of rock and rollers, but these new stars were baby boomers. They had different experiences and expectations.

Sexism and traditional gender discrimination remained in place throughout society in the 1960s, however. Women did not have equal rights with men even though they were playing larger roles in many areas, including the pop music business. This was obvious to those who worked in the Brill Building in New York City.

Home to more than 160 music businesses that created, published, recorded, and promoted pop music, the Brill Building was a modernized version of Tin Pan Alley. The songwriters and record producers who worked in the building catered to the desires of millions of teenage baby boomers by creating memorable dance music and songs about love and broken hearts.

Although the music business had long been dominated by men, in this new era, three of the most celebrated Brill Building tunesmiths were young women. Carole King, Cynthia Weil, and Ellie Greenwich were married to their writing partners, Gerry Goffin, Barry Mann, and

Jeff Barry, respectively. Many of the songs written by the husband-wife teams of the Brill Building were number 1 hits recorded by "girl groups," which included both black singers and white singers.

It was the Goffin-King song "Will You Love Me Tomorrow" that launched the girl group industry in January 1961. The song was recorded by four young black women who had formed a group called the Shirelles several years earlier, when they were in junior high school. It was the first number 1 song in history by a girl group. King was barely out of high school herself, just 18 when she wrote the lyrics to "Will You Love Me Tomorrow." After the first hit by the Shirelles, Goffin-King hits dominated pop radio. The duo composed songs about dance crazes, such as Little Eva's "The Loco-Motion" and

The Shirelles launched female pop groups in the 1960s with their hit "Will You Love Me Tomorrow."

SURFING SONGS AND STRAWBERRY FIELDS 39

girl group classics about love and longing, such as the Chiffons' "One Fine Day."

Motown

The Brill Building was not the only hit factory in early-1960s America. In Detroit, Michigan, black songwriter Berry Gordy Jr. founded the Motown Record Corporation in 1959. Gordy assembled teams of songwriters, producers, musicians, singers, and record promoters who worked in a small bungalow marked only by a sign that said "HITSVILLE, U.S.A." Gordy's goal was to reach all teenagers, regardless of race.

Some of Motown's biggest early hits were written and produced by the songwriting brothers Brian and Eddie Holland, who teamed up with Lamont Dozier. These men, known as Holland-Dozier-Holland, came to define the Motown sound, writing and producing songs with popping rhythms, catchy hooks, soulful lead singers, and soaring background harmonies.

The songs of Holland-Dozier-Holland were the driving force behind the Motown girl group success of the Supremes, composed of singers Florence Ballard, Mary Wilson, and Diana Ross. The Supremes, who grew up together in the same Detroit housing project, went on to become one of the best-selling pop groups of the 1960s. Their hits included "You Can't Hurry Love," "Baby Love," "Come See About Me," "Stop! In the Name of Love," and "You Keep Me Hanging On."

Holland-Dozier-Holland wrote a string of pop and soul hits for other Motown superstars, including the Four Tops songs, "Baby I Need Your Loving," "I Can't Help Myself," and "Reach Out (I'll Be There)." They also wrote Marvin Gaye's songs "Can I Get a Witness" and "How Sweet It Is (To Be Loved By You)."

Smokey Robinson was another talent at Motown. He wrote pop hits for the Temptations, such as "My Girl," and a string of number one songs—including "You've Really Got a Hold on Me" and "The Tracks of My Tears"—for his own band, Smokey Robinson and the Miracles. Robinson sang in a soulful falsetto, and his songs explored romance and heartbreak with clever turns of phrase.

Between 1961 and 1971, Motown had 110 top 10 hits written by Robinson, Holland-Dozier-Holland, Gaye, and others.

Beatlemania

Motown hits might have been the sound of young America, but they were heard around the world, including in England, where one of the most influential bands of all time was starting to take shape. As *Rolling Stone* wrote, "No band has influenced pop culture the way the Beatles have. They were one of the best things to happen in the twentieth century, let alone the Sixties."[24] In 1961, the Beatles, a bar band in Liverpool, England, played live sets of hits by artists such as Little Richard, Chuck Berry, and Buddy Holly. In 1962, they were discovered by Brian Epstein, a record store manager who became the Beatles' manager. He saw them perform live and knew they were a special group. Epstein sent out tape recordings of their songs, eventually getting them a recording contract with Parlophone. Epstein also was responsible for the trademark Beatles look—they were originally wearing tight jeans and leather jackets, but Epstein suggested the collarless gray suits and shaggy haircuts. More changes were made to the band at Parlophone. Producer George Martin suggested a more polished drummer. At this time, Pete Best was their drummer, but Martin suggested Ringo Starr, adding him to the the final lineup of guitarist John Lennon, bassist Paul McCartney, and lead guitarist George Harrison.

The Beatles wrote their own songs, and their catchy tunes made them major pop stars in England in early 1963. With the Beatles, it became an expectation for bands to write their own music instead of performing hits written by songwriting teams such as those in the Brill Building. By December, they had a number 1 hit in the United States with "I Want To Hold Your Hand," which went platinum, selling more than 1 million copies in a few days. This set off Beatlemania, a term invented by the press to describe the intense adoration the Beatles inspired in their fans.

When the group made its first American TV appearance on *The Ed Sullivan Show* on February 9, 1964, millions of Americans watched. As John, Paul, George, and Ringo shook their long, shaggy hair and sang, "She loves you, yeah, yeah, yeah,"[25] TV cameras showed teenage girls shrieking hysterically in the audience. By April, the Beatles had surpassed Elvis Presley's record-setting sales achievements with 14 songs on the Billboard Hot 100 chart.

Lennon and McCartney were the primary songwriters for the Beatles, and they rarely composed songs based on the 12-bar blues form typically heard in rock music. Instead, their songs were built on complex chord patterns played on the guitar with seventh

The Beatles made their first TV appearance in America on The Ed Sullivan Show. *Teenage girls in the audience screamed with excitement during their performance.*

chords used for a blues feel, minor chords used to create a moody sound, and jazz chords inserted to add a unique harmony. Their melodies ascend to high points that excite the listener, and their lyrics often use clever or humorous wordplay, such as those in their song "A Hard Day's Night."

The Beatles never copied their musical accomplishments from album to album. Each LP was sure to be a surprise, sounding completely different than the one before. Within the first three years of their success, they released seven albums containing enduring hits such as "Yesterday," "Ticket to Ride," "We Can Work It Out," and "I Want to Hold Your Hand."

POP MUSIC: CHART-TOPPERS THROUGHOUT HISTORY

The Beatles let their creativity run wild in the recording studio, where they used string quartets, the Indian sitar, and French horns, instruments never before heard in rock music. Along with their brilliant producer George Martin, the group invented new sounds by tinkering with tape recorders and other electronic gadgets.

"Strawberry Fields Forever"

The Beatles were the first British pop group to have major success in the United States, and their popularity caused a wave called the British Invasion. Suddenly, previously unknown British groups such as the Dave Clarke Five, Peter and Gordon, the Animals, and Herman's Hermits had number 1 hits in America. The Rolling Stones began their career as a British Invasion band, achieving their first success in 1965 with "(I Can't Get No) Satisfaction."

Around 1966, the British Invasion was replaced by another kind of revolution. America was in a period of social upheaval that became known as the counterculture, or hippie, movement. Millions of baby boomers began to question accepted beliefs in their own lives and those held by society at large. They adopted their own slang and fashions that included long hair on both men and women, tie-dyed shirts, and blue jeans. These young adults, including pop stars such as the Beatles and Rolling Stones, began experimenting with marijuana and lysergic acid diethylamide (LSD, or acid). LSD was at the root of the hippie counterculture. While most people took the drug for enjoyment, it caused some users to experience paranoia and anxiety. It also caused users to experience auditory and visual hallucinations, which provided inspiration for some musicians. As a result of this intense, drug-fueled examination, many hippies became anti-war, anti-authority, and critical of powerful corporations.

In February 1967, the Beatles released a single that was unmatched in pop history. John Lennon wrote "Strawberry Fields Forever" during a period when he was experimenting with LSD, and the song is a dreamlike kaleidoscopic trip of swirling sounds. Lennon and George Martin created the song with layers of cellos, keyboards, backward cymbals, and a multi-stringed Indian instrument called a *swarmandal*. "Strawberry Fields Forever" showed that the Beatles, who were the biggest pop stars in the world, were making music that was experimental, varied, progressive, and beyond classification.

POP MUSIC IN THE MOVIES

Elvis starred in more than 30 movies in his career, but he was not the only pop star of the 1960s to become a movie star. In 1964, the Beatles starred in their movie, *A Hard Day's Night*, a musical comedy which details several days of the band members' lives during the height of Beatlemania. *Help!* is a fictional movie in which Ringo gains possession of a sacrificial ring that he cannot remove from his finger, resulting in the band being chased by cult members and the police through London, the Bahamas, and the Australian Alps. In 2016, a found-footage documentary film, *Eight Days a Week*, featured music, interviews, and stories of the Beatles from 1963 to 1966.

In 2007, the musical movie *Across the Universe* was released. Set in the 1960s, it tells the story of a group of young adults during the Vietnam War and how the draft and the anti-war movement affects them. The story is told through the music of the Beatles. In 2008, *Mamma Mia!*, a film based on the Broadway musical that is told through ABBA songs, was released. In 2018, the sequel, *Mamma Mia! Here We Go Again* was released.

The story of pop group Frankie Valli and the Four Seasons was told in the musical *Jersey Boys*, which ran on Broadway from 2005 to 2017 and also had a touring company. The musical was also adapted into a film by Clint Eastwood in 2014, and the same actor who played Frankie Valli in the

Sgt. Pepper's Lonely Hearts Club Band

"Strawberry Fields Forever" was the warm-up for the Beatles' psychedelic LP, *Sgt. Pepper's Lonely Hearts Club Band*, released in June 1967. Kenneth Tynan, music critic of the respected *London Times*, said *Sgt. Pepper* was such a revolutionary, game-changing piece of music that the album represented a "decisive moment in the history of Western civilization."[26] While some might consider this statement overblown, the album undoubtedly changed the way pop music was produced and marketed.

Sgt. Pepper was one of the earliest concept albums, in which all the songs were based on a single idea or theme. On this album, the idea was that John, Paul, George, and Ringo were no longer the Beatles, but instead members of a fictional music group. The album contained several masterpieces such as "Lucy In the Sky With Diamonds," "Being For the Benefit of Mr. Kite!," and "A Day

Shows such as Jersey Boys tell a story based on a band's songs.

original Broadway show portrayed him in the movie. These movies show that even 50 years after the artists' music was popular, they still have a large fan base that continues to be interested in learning more about them.

in the Life." The lyrics of Harrison's "Within You Without You" discuss deep spiritual and philosophical concepts, while the music is a hypnotic mix of Indian instruments, such as the multi-string sitar and the tabla drums.

The album cover of *Sgt. Pepper* is as unique as the music. The Beatles are surrounded by dozens of life-size cardboard cutouts of famous people, including Bob Dylan, Communist philosopher Karl Marx, and actors James Dean, Marlon Brando, and Mae West. The lyrics were printed in the album insert—another first—so listeners could sing along.

Part of the Beatles' appeal was always that they were funny, down-to-earth guys who easily related to their fans. According to Larry Starr and Christopher Waterman, *Sgt. Pepper* took this concept to a new level:

[The] album was constructed to invite listeners' participation in an implied community. The

SURFING SONGS AND STRAWBERRY FIELDS

record is a clearly and cleverly organized performance that ... actually [addresses] its audience. The opening song, "Sgt. Pepper's Lonely Hearts Club Band," formally introduces the "show" to come and acknowledges the listeners with lines like "We hope you will enjoy the show" ... It [positions] the rock album as the creator of an audience community.[27]

Sgt. Pepper sold 30 million copies worldwide and 11 million copies in the United States. The album was on the Billboard 200 chart for 88 weeks in a row; for 15 of those weeks, the album was in the number 1 position. Overall, the album was on the chart for 175 weeks. In 2017, a 50th anniversary edition of the album was reissued and went to number 1 in England for more than 25 weeks. This gave the album the longest gap in history between its first week at the top of the charts and its most recent run at the top of the charts.

The record was revolutionary in another way. Before the album was released, the pop music business was driven by sales of 45 RPM singles. *Sgt. Pepper* showed that a piece of popular music could be longer than a three- to six-minute single and that a pop artist could create a musical masterpiece that filled an entire album. As a result, LP albums became the dominant method of marketing music in the aftermath of *Sgt. Pepper*.

The End of the Beatles

In 1968, the Beatles formed their own record label, Apple. However, with the exception of the Beatles' own music, the label was a failure. The band itself, however, was still incredibly popular, and in 1969, they released one of their most-loved and acclaimed albums, *Abbey Road*. The album had an iconic cover that is frequently referenced in pop culture, and the location is a popular spot for Beatles fans, who recreate the cover pose and leave graffiti on the wall nearby.

Shortly after the success of *Abbey Road*, the band started to fall apart. Lennon and McCartney frequently argued, there were disagreements among the band members, and the stress of being a band that voiced a generation began to wear them down. In 1970, the Beatles officially disbanded, with each member going on to produce solo albums. McCartney and Starr still record music and tour as of 2018 and even collaborate on each other's music.

In 1980, tragedy struck when John Lennon was murdered by a fan outside the Dakota apartment

A section of Central Park was named "Strawberry Fields" as a memorial to John Lennon. Fans often leave tokens such as flowers on the "Imagine" mosaic as a tribute to him.

building across from Central Park in New York City. A section of Central Park across from the Dakota is named Strawberry Fields to memorialize him. Lennon's wife, Yoko Ono, landscaped that part of the park in Lennon's honor. Inside of the Strawberry Fields section of the park is a mosaic with the word "Imagine" after Lennon's song of the same name, which is about imagining that the things that divide people do not exist. In 2001, fans were devastated again when Harrison died of cancer.

The Impact of the Beatles

Some of the most influential bands in pop music shaped the 1960s. The Beatles broke records and changed the sound of pop music. They even changed how it was marketed from that point forward with influential albums such as *Sgt. Pepper's Lonely Hearts Club Band*. Even in the 2000s, reissues or new greatest hits albums still appear on the charts, showing that pop bands can have staying power and still speak for the current generation, even 50 years after the height of their careers.

CHAPTER THREE

The Rise of Pop Icons

With the end of the Beatles, new supergroups such as the Jackson 5, ABBA, and the Bee Gees took over and are still influential today, whether their music is sung on a TV show, played in a movie, or has a Broadway show and movie based around it. In the 1980s, pop music got a major boost from iconic artists who still influence the musicians of today. Musicians such as Madonna and Michael Jackson have forever changed the music industry. However, album sales are not the only reasons for these artists' fame—they have inspired fashion trends as well as raised awareness for global social causes, showing that pop stars can have an even more lasting impact than just their music.

The Jackson 5

In 1969, the Jackson 5 became a pop music worldwide sensation. This is somewhat remarkable because Berry Gordy of Motown Records was hesitant to sign them due to their young ages—Michael had not even turned 10 by the time they were signed to a recording contract. However, he saw something special in Michael and decided to sign them. Made up of brothers Tito, Jackie, Marlon, Jermaine, and Michael, the group became famous thanks to their first album, *Diana Ross Presents the Jackson 5*. The album had hits such as "I Want You Back" and "Who's Loving You," which sold 2 million copies in 6 weeks. The band went to number 1 on the pop charts, making them one of the biggest pop groups in history. In 1970, their first four singles went straight to number 1—"ABC," "I Want You Back," "I'll Be There," and "The Love You Save." In 1971, they even had their own cartoon show, coloring books, posters, and more. In 1972, they broke the fan attendance record that was previously set by the Beatles at the Liverpool Empire Theater. The group had wide appeal which "was more than just musical—they were among the first black teen idols to appeal to a white audience. The Jackson 5's mix of mind-blowing musical talent and sheer charisma earned the family the status of pop royalty in the music business and later helped Michael's legendary solo career."[28]

In 1972, Michael and Jermaine both released solo albums, and their music started to reflect current trends as well as the oldest members' transition into adulthood. In 1976, their contract with Motown expired, and they moved to Epic, changing their name to "The Jacksons" at the same time. This same year, Jermaine left the band and youngest brother Randy took his place. In 1979, 10 years after their first album, the Jacksons finally had complete artistic control of an album, which worked extremely well for them—"Shake Your Body (Down to the Ground)," which was written by Michael and Randy, sold more than 2 million copies and stayed on the Black Singles Chart

The Jackson 5's members were teen idols. The band experienced success for more than 10 years and launched Michael Jackson's solo career.

THE RISE OF POP ICONS 49

for 23 weeks. It was the band's first multi-platinum single and would be their best-selling single, with more than 2.5 million sold. Around this time, Michael's solo career really began to take off, solidifying his future as a solo artist rather than a member of the Jackson 5. His album *Off the Wall*, released in 1979, sold 20 million copies worldwide. In 1984, Michael finally left the band after its *Victory* album and tour. In 1989, the Jacksons released *2300 Jackson Street*. It did not come close to the success of their previous albums, and they went on hiatus. In 2001, the group got together again for a celebration of Michael's solo career and toured for its 50th anniversary in 2015.

The Bee Gees

Formed by brothers Barry, Robin, and Maurice Gibb, the Bee Gees had a more than 40-year career and sold more than 200 million albums worldwide. However, their music went largely unnoticed between 1962, when their first album was released, and 1967. In this five-year span, they released two albums and a dozen singles, and they even wrote their own music. It was not until 1967, with the release of their song "New York Mining Disaster 1941," that they had a top 20 hit in England and America. After this, they had a series of popular hits, such as "I Started a Joke," "To Love Somebody," and "I've Got to Get a Message to You." Additionally, Robin

FLEETWOOD MAC

Fleetwood Mac is another British-American supergroup that started in the 1960s and rose to prominence in the 1970s. The group was originally formed by drummer Mick Fleetwood, bassist John McVie, and John's wife, keyboardist Christine McVie. The group found mainstream success in 1975 when they added two American songwriters, singer Stephanie "Stevie" Nicks and her boyfriend, guitarist Lindsey Buckingham.

The band had hits such as "Go Your Own Way," "Don't Stop," "Rhiannon," and "Dreams." Before the band went on hiatus in 1982, Fleetwood Mac produced a string of number-1 hits that dominated FM radio. The group's 1977 *Rumours* album sold more than 40 million copies and is one of the top 10 best-selling albums in history.

tried a solo career between 1969 and 1970, and Barry and Maurice recorded albums as a duo. However, shortly after achieving success, they had a series of albums between 1971 and 1975 that did poorly.

In 1975, producer Arif Mardin was recruited, and he "steered them to the funk-plus-falsetto combination that brought them their third round of hits,"[29] such as "Nights on Broadway," and "Jive Talkin.'" In the mid–1970s, manager Robert Stigwood asked the Bee Gees to record four to five songs for a soundtrack of a new movie he was producing, *Saturday Night Fever*, starring John Travolta. The film and soundtrack were immensely popular and gave the Bee Gees some of their greatest hits, "Night Fever," "How Deep Is Your Love," and "Stayin' Alive." The album hit number 1 and was on the charts for more than two years, selling 30 million copies worldwide. By 1979, the Bee Gees had more than 20 hit songs and 5 platinum records. However, with all this success came a backlash against the band for its disco-pop music and overplay of the songs on the radio. Following a lawsuit against Stigwood and solo work with other artists, the brothers reunited in 1987 for *E-S-P*. The album did not do well in the United States, but it was number 1 in Germany, and in the United Kingdom (UK), the album was in the top 5. This started the next phase of the group's career, in which their music became popular and hit the charts everywhere except in the United States. In 1997, the Bee Gees were inducted into the Rock & Roll Hall of Fame. In 2003, Maurice Gibb died of cardiac arrest, and in 2012, Robin Gibb died of cancer.

ABBA

As the Rock & Roll Hall of Fame stated, "ABBA made waves in the pop culture of the seventies that still resonate today."[30] The Swedish pop group, made up of Agnetha Fältskog, Björn Ulvaeus, Benny Andersson, and Anni-Frid Lyngstad, has sold more than 350 million singles and albums worldwide and "were the first group from a non-English speaking country to have consistent success in English speaking countries."[31] Named for the first initial of each member's first name, the band won a song contest in 1974 with their song "Waterloo." About a year and a half after the contest, they had another hit with the song "SOS" and went on to have worldwide success.

ABBA topped charts and broke records in France, England, Germany, Italy, Holland, and

EXPANSION OF THE MUSIC INDUSTRY

In the early years of pop, the most innovative music was promoted by small, independent labels such as Motown and Sun Records. During the 1970s, profits generated by pop music attracted the attention of executives at major media corporations. By 1973, the independent labels were largely gone, consumed by six major entertainment corporations: Columbia/CBS, RCA, MCA, Capitol-EMI, Polygram, and Warner. These companies controlled 90 percent of the record business, which generated $2 billion in profits. This figure was almost twice as much as movie industry profits in 1973 and three times more than professional sports.

Growth in the music business was fueled by a new way to sell music: prerecorded tapes. Eight-track and cassette tapes had been introduced in the 1960s, but by the mid-1970s, they accounted for only one-third of music sales in America. In order to listen to music in their cars, millions of baby boomers bought albums on tape that they already owned on vinyl. Propelled by this phenomenon, record company profits doubled to $4 billion by 1978.

Scandinavia. In the UK, the group had 19 top 10 singles, 8 of which went to number 1, between 1974 and 1982. In the United States, however, the group only hit the top 10 list 4 times and had a number-1 hit once with "Dancing Queen" in 1977. However, 20 of their songs have made it on the Hot 100, with 8 of their albums being certified platinum or gold by the RIAA. Additionally, "from 1975 to 1980, ABBA spent 43 weeks atop Britain's album charts—a feat equaled by no one."[32]

ABBA mania did not fully kick in throughout the United States until the musical Mamma Mia! arrived on Broadway in 2001. The musical was written by Björn and Benny, and by late 2009, the musical had been performed 3,400 times. By 2016, it had been seen by more than 60 million people. The 2008 film Mamma Mia! and the 2018 sequel, Mamma Mia! Here We Go Again further fueled ABBA mania, which is even more remarkable considering that the band split up in 1982. The musical and film popularized the songs that were number-1 hits in the UK, such as "Mamma Mia," "Take a Chance on Me," "Super Trouper," and "Dancing Queen."

In 2010, the band was inducted into the Rock & Roll Hall of Fame, and a touring exhibition called ABBAWORLD opened in London the same year. In May 2013, the exhibition was given a permanent home in Stockholm, Sweden, and

ABBA had huge success and broke records that not even the Beatles accomplished. The United States did not truly experience ABBA mania until the musical Mamma Mia! *became extremely popular, followed by the film of the same name several years later.*

it has had more than 1 million visitors as of 2016. The museum has costumes the band wore and other items the band members donated, along with personal videos, wax figures, and replicas of important places where the band members lived or worked during their career. The band has gotten together for events but always denied that they would tour or make new music together—they wanted fans to remember them as they were at the height of their careers when they were younger. However, on April 27, 2018, the band announced that they had recorded two new songs together and that it felt good to record again.

MTV

The world of pop music changed forever on August 1, 1981, though few noticed at the time. At one minute after midnight, a new cable TV channel launched in northern New Jersey. The cable channel was called Music Television, or MTV. The station ushered in a new era in pop music, one that still continues to this day. Only a few

THE RISE OF POP ICONS

thousand people viewed the launch of MTV, but within two years, the channel was available in most American cities and suburbs. The popularity of MTV was unprecedented and quickly began driving the record sales of bands shown in music videos. In June 1983, even the serious news reporter Ted Koppel took notice, telling viewers that MTV "has done wonders for the sagging record industry. It has made overnight stars of rock groups ... It uses some of the most creative visual and editing techniques seen on television ... [You] may not have yet seen it, musical video tapes ... set to slick, sometimes bizarre, choreography. It's a bonanza for singers, dancers, musicians, and the record industry."[33]

The King of Pop

MTV was designed to appeal to white suburban teenagers. For the first 18 months of its existence, MTV refused to play clips by black artists such as Rick James, whose album *Street Songs* had gone triple-platinum. Facing charges of racism, the channel decided to air Michael Jackson's video for "Billie Jean" in March 1983. Jackson recorded his first solo album in 1972 and was a major solo star by 1979, when his album *Off the Wall* sold more than 20 million copies.

By the time his sixth solo album, *Thriller*, was released in November 1982, the 24-year-old singer was a perfect fit for MTV. Jackson looked good, he could dance like no one else, and *Thriller* appealed to a broad demographic. The song "Beat It" had a funky dance beat that was popular in clubs. It featured a gritty guitar solo by hard-rock maestro Eddie Van Halen, of the rock group Van Halen. Another *Thriller* single, "The Girl Is Mine," features Jackson singing with Paul McCartney. The duet with a former Beatle attracted millions of baby boomers to the record.

Within a year of its release, *Thriller* sold more than 10 million copies in the United States alone and went on to sell more than 100 million, making it the best-selling album in history. The album was still breaking records in 2015, with more than 30 million copies sold in the United States. The RIAA certified the album as 30 times multi-platinum. Some of this success was driven by Jackson's video clips. "Billie Jean," the first video by a black artist to receive regular play on MTV, shows Jackson at his finest. He spins, jumps, and slides with a grace and style unmatched by any other dancer on MTV. Jackson's look was also new. He was dressed in a glittery black jacket, pink shirt, and red bowtie. Within weeks, students across America were imitating Jackson's look. Jackson's next video, "Beat It," was even more popular. The video was directed by Broadway choreographer Michael Peters and cost more than $150,000 to make. Tom McGrath wrote, "What made it great was the dancing. Michael, dressed in a red leather jacket, snapped and stepped and shrieked to the music, this time with more than 100 talented extras moving along with him. Never before had there been a video like this one. Almost single-handedly, this shy former child star had taken the entire field of music video and lifted it up a notch artistically."[34]

However, the most iconic music video of Michael Jackson's was the one for "Thriller," which cost around $500,000 to create. It was directed by John Landis, who also directed the horror movie *An American Werewolf in London*, and featured a spoken-word part by Vincent Price, a famous actor in horror movies such as 1953's *House of Wax* and 1959's *House on Haunted Hill*. The nearly 14-minute music video starts out with Jackson on a date with a girl. Then, their car runs out of gas, and the couple has to walk to their destination. As Jackson is talking with his date and a cloud uncovers the full moon, Jackson starts turning into a werewolf. Eventually, it is shown that the couple is at a movie theater watching a movie called *Thriller*. They walk out of the theater and down the road as the song kicks in. After the couple walks by the cemetery, zombies start coming out of the ground and buildings, surrounding Jackson and his date as it is revealed that Jackson is also a zombie. Jackson and the zombies put on a memorable dance number that still amazes fans decades after it was created. In 2009, it was the first music video inducted into the Library of Congress's National Film Registry, and it set the standard for music videos that came after, even though most people believe no music video has come close to the storytelling of "Thriller." As of 2018, it remains the only music video to be inducted into the registry. Michael Jackson impacted pop music in a way that few artists have been able to since. John Branca and John McClain, co-executors of Michael Jackson's estate, said, "There has never been a phenomenon like *Thriller*."[35]

By 1984, Jackson was known as the King of Pop. He further solidified that title with albums such as *Bad* in 1987 and *Dangerous* in 1991. However, throughout the 1990s, his reputation was damaged by his eccentric and secluded lifestyle at his home and ranch,

THE RISE OF POP ICONS

The music video for "Thriller," shown here, remains one of the most celebrated music videos in history.

called Neverland. Further damage was done by accusations of child molestation. He remained a celebrity internationally, but it was hard for him to recover his image in the United States. In 2001, he was inducted into the Rock & Roll Hall of Fame, but in 2003, he was charged with child molestation again. In 2005, he was found not guilty but faced financial difficulties in the aftermath. In 2009, he was hoping to make a comeback and was preparing for a series of concerts. However, on June 25, 2009, he died of cardiac arrest, which was ruled a homicide from a combination of sedatives in November of that year. His personal physician was found guilty of involuntary manslaughter in November 2011.

Rhythm Nation

In the early 1980s, Michael was not the only Jackson with an impressive pop music career. His youngest sister, Janet, released albums in 1982 and 1984, although both albums were unremarkable. Following these albums, she developed her own style and sound and released *Control* in 1986. The album had two songs—"Nasty" and "What Have You Done for Me Lately"—that hit the top 10. Janet Jackson is a powerful, independent woman, and that has resonated with fans since her breakthrough album.

In 1989, she released her most diverse album, the fan favorite *Janet Jackson's Rhythm Nation 1814*. This album gave Jackson seven top 10 hits, such as "Love Will Never Do (Without You)" and "Miss You Much." From this point, Jackson continued to release hit albums that were loved by both fans and critics, such as 1993's *janet.*, 1995's *Design of a Decade*, 1997's *The Velvet Rope*, and 2001's *All for You*.

In 2004, Jackson was the center of controversy following her Super Bowl performance with Justin Timberlake. During the show, Timberlake accidentally ripped the front of her costume, exposing Jackson's breast on live TV. She immediately covered herself with a look of shock on her face. However, in the end, Jackson took the blame and the heaviest hit for the incident, even though it was unplanned and unintentional. Timberlake joked about the incident, saying that he and Jackson loved giving people things to talk about, and in a taped apology, she accepted responsibility for her shirt ripping. As a result, Jackson was barred from attending both the Grammy Awards and MTV Video Music Awards while Timberlake was able to attend without a problem. As of 2018, Jackson has not had a single song reach the top 10 since the 2004 Super Bowl. In 2015, Jackson released her first album since 2008 and performed a 56-date *State of the World* tour in 2017. The album was appropriately titled *Unbreakable*, and it was widely praised.

It took Jackson years to get her career back on track while Timberlake released three acclaimed albums between the 2004 Super Bowl and 2015. In 2018, Timberlake released his fourth

Janet Jackson's career was temporarily derailed in 2004, but her talent remained undeniable, leading to a comeback.

solo album, *Man of the Woods*, and performed again at the Super Bowl. When it was announced that he would be the performer at the 2018 Super Bowl halftime show, #JusticeForJanet spread across Twitter, with users calling attention to the double standards for men and women in society: Jackson not only had to deal with having her body exposed on TV, she was also shamed for the incident, even though she had no control over it. They criticized the fact that Timberlake was asked to perform again at the Super Bowl while Jackson still dealt with backlash from the events of 2004. Twitter users even rebranded the day of the 2018 Super Bowl as #JanetJacksonAppreciationDay. Throughout the day, users posted clips of some of her most memorable performances and achievements to show support for her, and it was a trending topic on Twitter on the day of the game.

In 2018, Jackson headlined the *ESSENCE* festival in New Orleans, Louisiana. With a career that spans more than four decades, Jackson continues to be a powerful icon in pop music.

SYNTHESIZERS

Electric guitars made the sound of rock and roll possible in the 1950s and expanded the range of pop music in the 1960s. In the 1980s, the synthesizer keyboard played a role comparable to the electric guitar in previous decades. The Yamaha DX7, introduced in 1983, was the first commercially successful digital synthesizer. The electronic instrument can produce a wide range of sounds that imitate piano, organ, woodwinds, brass, strings, bass, and drums. Synthesizers can also be programmed to combine these sounds with unusual electronic effects unlike any produced by traditional instruments.

Madonna: Queen of Pop

Michael Jackson's success earned him the title the King of Pop. In the mid-1980s, he shared his reign with the Queen of Pop, Madonna Louise Ciccone, known simply as Madonna. Born in a Detroit, Michigan, suburb in 1958, Madonna studied dance, singing, and drumming in her teen years. In 1983, Madonna had her first major breakthrough with the platinum album *Madonna*, filled with up-tempo songs featuring synthesizers and disco drumbeats.

Madonna achieved a level of control and power that was unprecedented for women in the music industry at that time. She cultivated a confrontational sound

Madonna is one of the most influential female pop stars in music history. She broke records and became a powerful figure in the music business.

and a look calculated to capitalize on the MTV road to stardom. She fully took advantage of the benefits of the music video in the early 1980s, creating distinctive, controversial images. In January 1984, she appeared on the popular TV show *American Bandstand*, telling the host Dick Clark that she wanted "to rule the world."[36] By the end of the year, Madonna's bold statement had come true. Her dance-pop 1985 album *Like a Virgin* hit number 1 on the Billboard chart, and by the end of 1985, *Like a Virgin* had sold 5 million copies. It was the first album by a female artist to receive this honor.

Musically, *Like a Virgin* was in a style called new wave, which melded disco, rock, sixties pop, and synthesizer, or synth-based, electronic music. Produced by Nile Rodgers, one of the pioneers of 1970s disco, singles from the album such as "Angel," "Material Girl," and "Like a Virgin" were light, catchy, and easy to dance to.

By 1991, Madonna had 21 top-10 hits and had sold more

than 70 million albums worldwide. In addition, she signed a $60 million deal with Time-Warner, becoming head of the Maverick division of the company. In 1998, she released *Ray of Light*, which was a success with both critics and fans. This album earned Madonna her first Grammy Award for music, whereas her previous awards had been for music videos. In 2000, she released *Music*, and in 2005, she released *Confessions on a Dance Floor*. On 2008's *Hard Candy*, she worked with artists such as Justin Timberlake, Pharrell Williams, and Timbaland to create a unique, hip-hop inspired album. Also in 2008, she was inducted into the Rock & Roll Hall of Fame. Madonna continues to be an icon and push boundaries. In 2015, she released *Rebel Heart*, and in 2017, she marched with thousands at the Women's March on Washington (a worldwide protest to advocate for women's rights, reproductive rights, immigration rights, and more) and spoke at the event, proving that she is an important force in the fight for human rights as well as the music industry.

New Kids on the Block

In the 1960s, the Beatles had the attention of thousands of screaming, adoring fans. In the 1970s, it was the Jackson 5. In 1989, New Kids on the Block arrived on the pop music scene and foreshadowed the arrival of boy bands in the 1990s. In fact, it was New Kids on the Block that inspired the creation of boy bands such as the Backstreet Boys, and these bands changed the face of pop music forever.

New Kids on the Block was made up of brothers Jordan and Jonathan Knight, Donnie Wahlberg, Joey McIntyre, and Danny Wood. Their first album in 1986 did not crack the Billboard 200 when it was released, but their 1988 follow-up album *Hangin' Tough* earned them five top 10 hits on the Billboard Hot 100 in 1989, including their first number 1 hit, "I'll Be Loving You (Forever)," which was followed by popular hits "Please Don't Go Girl" and "You Got It (The Right Stuff)."

The group's third album was a holiday album titled *Merry, Merry Christmas*. When this album was released, songs from their second album continued to be Billboard hits, and the band was soon a merchandising and touring powerhouse, making more money than Michael Jackson and Madonna. In 1990, they released their fourth album *Step by Step*. The title song and the album earned the band Hot 100 and Billboard

New Kids on the Block greatly influenced the creation of later boy bands. They were a huge hit with teenage fans in the late 1980s and early 1990s. Their initial success was short-lived, but they experienced a minor revival in the late 2000s.

200 number 1 hits. New Kids on the Block was named the top artist of 1989 and 1990 by *Billboard*, but in the early 1990s, musical tastes started to change toward grunge and rap. Their 1994 album *Face the Music* hit a high of number 37 on the Billboard charts, and the band went on hiatus. They did not release another album until 2008's *The Block*, which hit number 2 on the Billboard charts. In addition, the song "Summertime" became their first top 40 hit since 1992.

In 2011, New Kids on the Block released a collaborative album with the Backstreet Boys, called *NKOTBSB*, and the two groups also went on tour together. In 2013, New Kids on the Block released the album *10*, which peaked at number 6 on the Billboard charts. After another four-year hiatus, they released *Thankful*, a five-track album, in 2017.

"The Right Stuff"

New Kids on the Block have accepted and solidified their position as a boy band in the pop music industry. Without them, there would not be bands such as Backstreet Boys, *NSYNC, or One Direction. While some boy bands experience huge success and disband after only a few albums, other bands such as New Kids on the Block and Backstreet Boys keep creating music their fans identify with, even more than 20 years after the height of the bands' careers, proving that they have the talent to keep making incredible music and the staying power to keep resonating with their fans.

CHAPTER FOUR

Tearin' Up Fans' Hearts:
Teen Pop of the 1990s

The early 1990s were a bad time for pop music. While the New Kids on the Block experienced success in 1990, once grunge and rap became popular, pop music's popularity waned. However, in the early 1990s, a new boy band was being put together, and once it arrived on the scene in the mid-1990s, it was larger than life. This band, called the Backstreet Boys, kicked off the next explosion of pop music that gave rise to many artists who are still making music in 2018.

"Spice Up Your Life"

Boy bands largely dominated the pop music scene in the 1990s; however, a girl group from Europe called the Spice Girls also took the world by storm, quickly rising to the top of the charts and becoming the most successful British band to come to North America since the Beatles. Each member of the group had a special spice name. In 1993, Geri Halliwell (Ginger Spice), Melanie Chisholm (Sporty Spice), Victoria Adams (Posh Spice), Melanie Brown (Scary Spice), and Emma Bunton (Baby Spice) responded to an advertisement looking for five female pop singers. The five women auditioned and worked well together.

In July 1996, their first single, "Wannabe," was released, and it went to number 1 in 30 countries. It was followed by "Say You'll Be There," and then the album *Spice* was released, which sold more than 20 million copies worldwide. In 1997, the Spice Girls debuted in the United States, and their second album, *Spiceworld,* was released later in the year. The album had hits such as "Spice Up Your Life,"

"Stop," and "Viva Forever." Along with the album, *Spice World: The Movie* was released. It was loved by fans but received poor reviews from critics.

In 1998, the group started to fall apart when Adams (Posh Spice) announced she was engaged to soccer star David Beckham. Following this, Halliwell (Ginger Spice) left the band in the middle of their 1998 tour. In 2000, the group released their final album, *Forever*, which ended with the song "Goodbye." Their time in pop music stardom was short-lived, but they captured fans' attention. Since they broke up, fans have been hoping for a reunion. The group performed at the closing ceremonies of the 2012 London Olympics. Then, in 2018, Brown (Scary Spice) stated that the Spice Girls would be reuniting, but Posh Spice (who changed her last name from Adams to Beckham after her marriage) shut down the possibility of a tour. Brown hinted that the Spice Girls would be at the royal wedding of Prince Harry and Meghan Markle. However, when the day came, there was no performance. Only three members of the band were invited, and only Beckham was seen in attendance, leaving fans to still wonder when, if ever, the pop music icons will perform together again.

Backstreet Boys: The Hysteria Begins

One of the most successful teen pop bands, the Backstreet Boys, was formed in 1993 in Orlando, Florida, by Lou Pearlman. Pearlman created an advertisement looking for teenage male singers, and out of this advertisement, Kevin Richardson, Nick Carter, Howie Dorough, Richardson's cousin Brian Littrell, and A. J. McLean came together as the Backstreet Boys. In 1994, they met with Johnny Wright, who was a road manager for New Kids on the Block. He arranged for them to go on promotional, unpaid tours across middle and high schools in America to get their name out. It was also Wright who suggested the Backstreet Boys go to Europe because there was a boy band movement occurring there at the time. It was this suggestion that changed their careers forever.

In 1995, the Backstreet Boys received a record deal with Jive Records and went to Europe to record with legendary producers Max Martin and Denniz Pop. Up to that time, the group had a different sound. As soon as they started working with Martin and Pop, their sound became distinctive, more edgy and electronic, which is especially clear on "We've Got It Goin' On." Following Wright's suggestion after recording their album, the band started touring in Europe and showing fans that they were different from other boy bands. As Carter stated in the *Backstreet Boys: Show 'Em What You're Made Of* documentary, "Our take was these bands are all lip syncing. So [we'll] go on stage and sing for real and show them something they've never seen before."[37] This tactic proved extremely successful—their first self-titled album sold millions of copies in Europe. In addition, they got a sign of things to come: Fans would surround them, crawling on top of and around their buses, making them unable to easily get out of the area where they were parked. A new kind of band hysteria that resembled Beatlemania had begun.

Even though their first album was incredibly successful in Europe, the Backstreet Boys were still unknown in the United States. By 1997, their music was starting to be heard in Canada, but still not in the United States.

The Backstreet Boys experienced fame in Europe before coming back to the United States. Photos such as this one frequently appeared in teen magazines, and fans would hang them up on their wall or in their locker.

However, cities such as Buffalo, New York, and Detroit, Michigan, are close to the U.S.–Canada border, so these cities often pick up Canadian stations. Listeners were soon requesting these songs from Buffalo and Detroit radio stations. As Kevin said, "Cities like Buffalo and Detroit would hear the radio stations across the border. People were calling to request our songs, but the DJs were like, 'We don't know who they are!'"[38] However, pop music was starting to rise again in the United States thanks to songs such as the Spice Girls' "Wannabe" and Hanson's "MMMBop," and suddenly, seemingly overnight, the Backstreet Boys became a sensation in the United States. As Howie stated, "We were coming out of the Gulf War, America kinda needed something that was a little more uplifting. I think people just wanted to feel good again."[39]

Their debut album in America, *Backstreet Boys*, is one of the most successful debuts ever—on the Billboard charts, it reached number 4, and the RIAA certified the album as 14 times platinum. Many iconic hit songs that are still fan favorites came from this album, including "I'll Never Break Your Heart," "Quit Playing Games (With My Heart)," and "Everybody (Backstreet's Back)." "Everybody (Backstreet's Back)" was an especially big hit and had a video reminiscent of Michael Jackson's "Thriller," in which the Backstreet Boys end up at a mansion, turn into various creatures such as mummies, vampires, and werewolves, and perform a memorable dance. The Backstreet Boys performed this dance again many years later at the end of the James Franco, Jonah Hill, and Seth Rogen 2013 movie *This Is the End*. The Backstreet Boys were so popular that the record company wanted them back in the studio to start working on another album, keeping them in the spotlight. They had no idea of the level of hysteria that was to come.

"Larger Than Life"

"You are my fire / The one desire / Believe when I say / I want it that way."[40] Those words from the first single off of *Millennium*, "I Want It That Way," launched the Backstreet Boys into an even deeper level of fan hysteria they did not anticipate. The single was released on April 12, 1999, and the album was released May 18, setting the record for first week sales of an album with 1.1 million copies sold in the United States alone. McLean said, "The day that we released *Millennium* was a mind-boggling day for us in

The Backstreet Boys reached the height of their popularity in the late 1990s and early 2000s. The demands of fame, combined with personal issues, led them to take a hiatus.

history. They shut down Times Square ... it was nuts."[41] In December 1999, the group dominated the Billboard Music Awards and walked away with Album of the Year for *Millennium* and Artist of the Year.

The album launched even more hit songs for the Backstreet Boys, such as "Larger Than Life" and "Show Me the Meaning of Being Lonely." However, the record label wanted even more from them, and a year after releasing *Millennium*, the band released the first single off of *Black and Blue*, "The One," on May 16, 2000. In October, they released the second single, "Shape of My Heart," and on November 21, 2000, the album was released. However, because of how much the label was demanding of them, the band members were becoming exhausted from nonstop albums and touring. They were also dealing with personal issues, such as Littrell's open heart surgery in 1998 and McLean's alcohol and drug addiction. In 2001, a greatest hits album was released, and then they went on hiatus.

Backstreet's Back

In 2005, the band came back from hiatus and released *Never Gone*. In 2006, Richardson announced he was leaving the band to take a break from celebrity life, but the other four members of the group continued to make music. They released *Unbreakable* in 2007 and *This Is Us* in 2009. Around this time, they also started doing cruises, in which fans can go on a luxury boat trip with the band. They then recorded an album with New Kids on the Block and toured with them, and six years after leaving the band, Richardson returned for the making of a new album with the full Backstreet lineup. The album, *In a World Like This*, was released in 2013, debuting at number 5 on the Billboard 200. This album further broke records—with it, the band had 9 top 10 albums—the only boy band in music history to accomplish this feat.

In 2015, the band released a documentary film, *Backstreet Boys: Show 'Em What You're Made Of*, which showed the making of *In a World Like This* and also

The Backstreet Boys remained popular even after their hiatus. Demand for the band's music and shows remains high nearly 20 years after their fame peaked.

LOU PEARLMAN

Lou Pearlman is a name infamous among Backstreet Boys and *NSYNC fans. He was the music executive who was responsible for the creation of each band; however, he withheld royalties from the bands, keeping millions for himself and leaving the bands with very little to show for all they had accomplished. In the 1980s, he created a scam airline company to get money from investors. By the late 1980s, he became wealthy and saw how successful bands such as New Kids on the Block were. He decided to jump on the success of boy bands and create his own to make even more money. In 1992, he placed an advertisement that he was looking for teenage male singers.

The first band to be formed from this advertisement was the Backstreet Boys; they were signed to Pearlman's Trans Continental Records. Four years after this, seemingly overnight, they burst onto the pop music scene in the United States. Teenage fans loved the Backstreet Boys and, like the New Kids on the Block, they became merchandising and touring powerhouses. The problem was that Pearlman wanted more and more money, and he created more boy bands, such as *NSYNC, to compete with bands he already created and managed. Additionally, Pearlman and his executives kept $10 million in royalties for the Backstreet Boys alone, leaving them $300,000 to split among themselves. When the band confronted Pearlman, he made excuses, stating that he had spent millions to get them into the industry and had to make that back. He also stated he was like a sixth member of the band and therefore deserved one-sixth of their profits. However, what he was doing was illegal, and the Backstreet Boys sued him, resulting in a court case involving 20 lawyers and judges in 3 states.

The Backstreet Boys were the first band to sue, but not the only band—nearly every band that Pearlman managed, including *NSYNC, sued. In 2007, it was revealed that Pearlman had many fraudulent investments beyond his boy band scheme, and in 2008, he pleaded guilty to charges related to these investments. He received a prison sentence of 25 years, and he died in prison in 2016.

detailed the history of the band. In 2016, the band announced it was going to perform a residency, or a series of shows, in Las Vegas, Nevada, in 2017. The residency was renewed for 2018 because of how well it was doing, and the Backstreet Boys broke records once again with the fastest ticket sales for a Las Vegas residency show. In May 2018, the band released their first new song since 2007. The song, which is called "Don't Go Breaking My Heart," was an instant hit, debuting at number 32 on the charts.

The Backstreet Boys have affected pop music in a monumental way. They have broken records that not even the Beatles did and have proven that even after a hiatus and even after a member left for six years, they still have millions of fans supporting them and loving their music just as much as the first time they heard "As Long As You Love Me" or "Everybody (Backstreet's Back)."

*NSYNC

The boy band *NSYNC was the main competition for the Backstreet Boys in the late 1990s. The band formed in 1995, and much of its success took the same route as the Backstreet Boys. Lou Pearlman, manager of the Backstreet Boys, created them to be competition for the Backstreet Boys. Richardson of the Backstreet Boys said,

> *Around 1995, I came off the road, and Lou said, "Come here, I want to show you something," and he showed me a VHS tape of this group, they didn't have a name at the time, and I didn't know that it was a showcase that Lou had financed and Lou had been working with them. It was almost like a betrayal. You know, when we started out, we were like "Yeah, we're a team, we're gonna take over the world and there's nobody like us."*[42]

McLean of the Backstreet Boys said,

> *"We're molding them [NSYNC] in your image." That's what they told us ... I guess one wasn't enough, so now you've gotta have 15 boy groups? Next thing you know it's like, if we got tired and didn't want to tour, didn't want to do a certain TV show or whatever, *NSYNC was right there, picking up the pieces. Then, next thing you know, Jive Records signed *NSYNC. Lou basically created our competition.*[43]

Made up of members Justin Timberlake, Chris Kirkpatrick, Joey Fatone, Lance Bass, and J. C. Chasez—the last letters of their first names forming the group's initials (with Lance taking the nickname Lanceton after he replaced the original "n" in the group, Jason Galasso)—*NSYNC combined danceable beats and R&B harmonies into a formula for superstar success. Along with the Backstreet Boys, *NSYNC dominated the pop music scene, and just like the Backstreet Boys, they had success in Europe before coming back to the United States. In March 1998, *NSYNC's first self-titled album was released, launching the group into pop stardom. This was further fueled by a Disney channel concert special in July of that year. Max Martin worked on *NSYNC's debut just like he did for the Backstreet Boys, and once again, he created a unique sound that gathered millions of adoring fans. The album launched hits such as "(God Must Have Spent) A Little More Time on You," which hit number 8 on the Billboard charts, giving the group its first Billboard Top 10 in February 1998. Other hits to come off the album included "Tearin' Up My Heart," "I Want You Back," and "I Drive Myself Crazy." That same year, the band released a holiday album called *Home for Christmas*.

The group's 2000 album *No Strings Attached* is a little edgier than most teen pop offerings. It was originally supposed to be released in 1999; however, the group ran into legal troubles with Lou Pearlman. They were eventually able to end their contract with him and get signed to Jive Records.

*NSYNC was created to be the Backstreet Boys' competition, but many people became fans of both bands.

The legal battles with Pearlman influenced much of the album, marketing, and performances the group put on, which was most evident in their song "Bye, Bye, Bye." During performances and in music videos, they were portrayed as marionettes, or puppets on strings, who eventually broke free. Around this time, marionette dolls were released of each band member and were a hit for fans to add to their collection. The album sold 1 million copies on just the first day of its release, and by the end of the first week, nearly 2.5 million copies were sold.

Following *No Strings Attached*, the band went on tour in 2001 to promote the release of the album *Celebrity*. Once again, this album sold nearly 2 million copies by the end of the first week. It included hits such as "Pop," "Celebrity," and "Girlfriend." Many of the songs on the album were written by Timberlake and Chasez, a sign of what was to come. The band went on tour after the release of *Celebrity*, then went on hiatus in 2002 for Timberlake and Chasez to focus on solo careers. However, the hiatus became permanent, something that was not confirmed until 2007 by Lance Bass. Chasez's solo career did not take off, but Timberlake's solo career made him a pop music icon and one of the most famous names in pop music.

Britney Spears

Timberlake began his career in the early 1990s on the Disney Channel television show *The All-New Mickey Mouse Club*, which featured comedy skits and songs. The show also featured other cast members who went on to become superstars: actor Ryan Gosling, *NSYNC member J. C. Chasez, actress Keri Russell, and pop stars Britney Spears and Christina Aguilera, who both became famous around the same time.

Spears became a major pop sensation at the age of 16, when the single "…Baby One More Time" debuted in late 1998. The song was composed by Swedish music producer Max Martin, who also wrote chart-topping teen pop hits for the Backstreet Boys, *NSYNC, Katy Perry, and P!nk.

"…Baby One More Time" shot to number 1 as the video generated controversy over Spears's revealing costume and song lyrics. However, even throughout this controversy, the album was a hit with fans. The album *…Baby One More Time* quickly sold 10 million copies and eventually went on to sell more than 30 million. It included hits such as "(You Drive Me) Crazy" and "From the Bottom of My Broken Heart." In 2011, it was listed by *Guinness World Records* as the best-selling album by a

TRL

In 1998, MTV premiered the show *Total Request Live*, commonly called *TRL*. It aired daily with the top 10 music videos that were voted for by viewers in one of two ways: either on the website or by calling in to the station. Music videos were retired after a certain amount of time. The show featured a number of hosts throughout the years, such as Damien Fahey, but between 1998 and 2002, the show was hosted by Carson Daly, who became the most recognizable face of the show. The show was an important way for fans to connect with their favorite musicians or actors as well as for the musicians to connect with their fans; fans could sit inside or outside the studio in Times Square in New York City. Musicians would perform some of their songs and participate in interviews with the host. Famous pop music acts such as Backstreet Boys, *NSYNC, and Britney Spears were popular guests on the TV show, and the day the Backstreet Boys released *Millennium*, there were thousands of fans outside of the studio. In 2008, the show came to an end, although it was revived in 2017 with a different format.

Carson Daly (right), who was famously associated with TRL, *went on to host the reality singing competition* The Voice.

teenage solo artist. Spears's follow-up album, *Oops! ... I Did It Again*, broke records for solo artist album sales, selling 1.3 million copies in its first week. The follow-up album included bold, powerful songs such as "Stronger," "What U See (Is What U Get)," and "Lucky." Around this time, it was revealed that Spears and Timberlake had been dating since 1999. Many fans were deeply invested in their relationship, but the couple broke up in 2002. In 2001, Spears

Some of Britney Spears's achievements were recorded in the Guinness Book of World Records. *As of 2018, she is still making music and touring, proving that she is an unstoppable force in the pop music industry.*

personal life than her musical talents. In 2003, Spears released *In the Zone*, which launched the hit song "Toxic." The album sold nearly 3 million copies, and while her subsequent albums—such as 2007's *Blackout*, 2008's *Circus*, 2011's *Femme Fatale*, 2013's *Britney Jean*, and 2016's *Glory*—were important in pop music, they still suffered lower sales than she had been used to. Of her later albums, *Glory* has been the most praised and seen as a comeback for the pop star who initially caught fans' attention with "...Baby One More Time."

Avril Lavigne

During the 2000s, Spears was among the largest group of talented female singers in pop music history. Beyoncé, Christina Aguilera, Rihanna, P!nk, Katy Perry, and Kelly Clarkson, along with older artists such as Mariah Carey and Madonna, sold millions of

released her third album, *Britney*. After the release of this album and the end of her relationship with Timberlake, she again became the focus of controversy, with critics focusing more on her

TEARIN' UP FANS' HEARTS: TEEN POP OF THE 1990S

albums filled with dance pop, R&B, soul, and pop hits. The decade was also ripe for young female rockers, such as Canadian Avril Lavigne, who wanted to be recognized for their singing, songwriting, and guitar playing rather than their looks.

Lavigne was only 17 when she became famous. Unlike other pop stars who would wear glamorous, glittery costumes, Lavigne stayed true to herself by wearing jeans and tank tops, such as the outfit she wore in the video of her debut single "Complicated" in 2002. The song was released on the album *Let Go*, which quickly sold 6 million copies. Lavigne's appeal as an average girl instead of someone with a celebrity persona endeared her to millions worldwide when she appeared in the videos for "Complicated" and "Sk8r Boi." With *Let Go*, Lavigne became the youngest female musician to ever have a number-1 album in the UK. Her concert tour in support of the album took her to Australia, Asia, North America, and Europe, and *Let Go* was nominated for eight Grammys in 2003.

Despite her pop success, Lavigne was determined to be taken seriously as a singer and songwriter. Her second album, 2004's *Under My Skin*, dealt with issues such as depression and the death of her grandfather. The album went platinum within a month. In 2007, she released her third album, *The Best Damn Thing*. With the release of her fourth album, *Goodbye Lullaby*, in 2011, Lavigne continued to explore raw emotions and personal pain with mellow ballads such as "Goodbye," "Everybody Hurts," and "Wish You Were Here."

Like many other teen idols, Lavigne launched her own clothing line, called Abbey Dawn, and released three fragrances, *Black Star*, *Wild Rose*, and *Forbidden Rose*. However, she is also known for her charitable work. Lavigne promotes various environmental and humanitarian organizations, and in 2010, she launched the Avril Lavigne Foundation to help young people with serious illnesses and disabilities. In 2013, she released her fifth self-titled album. However, some people believe it is not really Lavigne who released the album—Lavigne has joined Elvis in the conspiracy theory world, and some people believe the real Avril Lavigne died and was replaced by a look-alike. Lavigne, of course, has denied the theory. In early 2018, she was releasing updates on her social media about a new album to be released that year, stating that it would go back to her roots.

Changes in Pop Music

Artists such as the Backstreet Boys, *NSYNC, and Britney Spears experienced widespread, record-breaking success in the 1990s and early 2000s. These artists changed the face of pop music forever, influencing future artists and allowing them to push boundaries themselves. Some artists, such as the Backstreet Boys and Britney Spears, continue making music more than 20 years after they first came on the pop music scene, while former *NSYNC member Justin Timberlake influences pop music more than he did within the boy band. Even though the height of boy bands and Britney Spears was in the 1990s and early 2000s, it paved the way for highly successful current-day artists such as Lady Gaga.

CHAPTER FIVE

An Ever-Changing *Art Form*

Pop music has had an incredible evolution—from the music of Tin Pan Alley and Elvis to the Beatles, the Backstreet Boys, and Kesha. It has taken on a new artistry and awareness of social issues that can be heard in the music of artists such as Lady Gaga. However, current pop music also has experienced controversy and backlash, along with questions about how socially aware pop music should be. Should it be pure entertainment? Should it discuss the struggles of current events? Is there a fine line that artists should walk to keep their fans and not alienate them? This argument has largely come into light with Justin Timberlake's *Man of the Woods* album, which was not as much of a hit as was anticipated and which did not discuss current events as much as some people wanted. However, even when pop stars encounter backlash, fans still count on their favorite artists to help get them through tough times and provide an escape as well as relatable feelings.

Justin Timberlake and the Tennessee Kids

Justin Timberlake is one of the biggest pop artists of the 2010s, and he has been one of the most-loved, most popular stars for more than 20 years. After *NSYNC's fourth album, Timberlake ventured out on a solo career, and the band said it was going on hiatus. However, Timberlake's solo career took off, so the hiatus remained permanent.

His first solo album, *Justified*, was released in 2002 and received a Grammy Award for Best Pop Vocal Album and Best Male Pop Vocal Performance for the song "Cry Me a River." The album included collaborations with Timbaland, the Neptunes, and Janet Jackson. While the album spawned hit singles such as "Like I Love You," "Señorita," and "Rock Your Body," the album was also praised for songs such as "Let's Take a Ride" and "Never Again" that a 2018 *Billboard* magazine article stated were not memorable but pleasing to go back and listen to even 16 years after the album was released. Following the release of this album, Timberlake toured with Christina Aguilera, who had just released her second album, *Stripped*. Four years later, in 2006, Timberlake released his even more successful follow-up album, *FutureSex/LoveSounds*, which received four Grammy Awards and generated fan favorites "My Love" and "SexyBack." Even with the wild success of his solo work, however, he was not treated as kindly by critics, who criticized the fact that Timberlake had not gone beyond the sweet bubblegum pop of *NSYNC's type of music.

Around this time, Timberlake started acting in movies. While artists are largely criticized for acting when their main career is singing or vice versa, Timberlake was praised for roles such as Sean Parker in 2010's *The Social Network*. Timberlake was also in the dramas *Alpha Dog* and *Black Snake Moan*, both released in 2006, and he starred in 2011's *Friends with Benefits* and *In Time*. Timberlake also became widely praised and loved for his *Saturday Night Live* skits. During this time, Timberlake had not released new music, and fans became anxious, wondering if their favorite singer would return to the career he originally became famous for. In 2013, fans got their answer with the release of *The 20/20 Experience*, an album that was released in two parts in the spring and fall of that year. Part one generated hits such as "Suit & Tie" (featuring JAY-Z) and "Mirrors," and part two included hits such as "Take Back the Night" and "Drink You Away." As the website Pitchfork wrote in its review, the album "seamlessly [combined] the last 40 years of pop, soul, and R&B into a series of ambitious, long songs."[44] While he was touring for these albums, he also starred in more movies, and during the final nights of the tour, his concerts were recorded for a Netflix concert film called *Justin Timberlake + the Tennessee Kids*. This gave fans the opportunity to relive their favorite moments from the tour and see behind the scenes. It also allowed fans who never had the opportunity to see Timberlake on tour to watch the show in their living rooms.

In 2016, Timberlake voiced a character in the animated movie *Trolls*, which was also famous for Timberlake's infectious dance-pop song "Can't Stop the Feeling,"

AN EVER-CHANGING ART FORM

and in 2017, he was in *Wonder Wheel*. In 2018, Timberlake finally released his first album in five years, *Man of the Woods*, and performed at the Super Bowl. This album was not as acclaimed as his previous works and also received backlash. Pitchfork, which praised *The 20/20 Experience*, stated that *Man of the Woods* was "a huge misstep for the pop star" because it "is musically and thematically shallow ... many of these tracks ... manage to overstay their welcome by a minute or two."[45] Jasmine Grant of the website *Bustle* wrote of the album,

> JT's lack of "wokeness" sticks out like a sore thumb in an era where music fans prefer their stars to come with a little social responsibility ... His [#WhyWeWearBlack] Instagram post the night of the 2018 Golden Globes was devoted to how "hot" his

*Justin Timberlake has been in the music business for more than 20 years between his role as an *NSYNC band member and a solo artist, and his popularity remains high.*

wife is ... rather than the rampant sexual misconduct in Hollywood (the reason celebrities were, in fact, wearing black). If you go back even further, JT has been noticeably hands-off about race related issues as well, like #BlackLivesMatter, Sandra Bland, Eric Garner, and Philando Castile which have dominated the media in recent years. This is especially troubling when you think about the fact that his catalogue of hits were made possible by black producers (i.e Timbaland and The Neptunes), musicians, and songwriters.[46]

The music video for "Supplies" off of *Man of the Woods* featured the #MeToo movement (an anti-harassment movement that supports survivors of sexual harassment and sexual assault and works to end sexual violence), police brutality, and the travel ban for people from certain countries in which the majority of the population is Muslim. Even with Timberlake acknowledging these issues, however, critics saw it as an attempt to stay relevant instead of him truly being an ally. Despite these criticisms, fans still scooped up Timberlake's *Man of the Woods* album—it earned him his fourth number 1 on the Billboard 200 chart, and his tour for the album was praised.

Joining him on the tour was his 15-piece band, which included a horn section. Unlike many artists who do not acknowledge their backing band or let them get into the music, Timberlake allows them to move around, dance, enjoy themselves, and have their own moment to shine. They are not just there to play his backing music; they are part of the show and even have their own name—the Tennessee Kids. Even though Timberlake's *Man of the Woods* album earned some backlash, he is still one of the most loved and celebrated pop stars in music history—one who has true staying power in the music business.

Beyoncé: Powerful Pop Superstar

Beyoncé Knowles-Carter is one of most successful music artists of all time. Born in Houston, Texas, in 1981, Beyoncé was destined for stardom. She began singing, dancing, and performing in talent shows at the age of 7. By high school, she had formed the group Destiny's Child, which topped the charts in 1999 with the album *The Writing's on the Wall*. It soon became clear to critics and the public alike that Beyoncé was the breakout star of Destiny's Child, thanks

Fans of Beyoncé sometimes call her Queen Bey, and the fan base often refers to itself as the Beyhive. They are some of the most devoted fans in today's pop scene.

POP MUSIC: CHART-TOPPERS THROUGHOUT HISTORY

JUSTIN BIEBER

Justin Bieber was only 12 when he began posting performance videos on YouTube. A video of an R&B song of his was accidentally discovered by an American talent scout named Scott "Scooter" Braun, who was searching for a different artist at the time. Braun was impressed enough to fly Bieber to Atlanta, Georgia, for an audition. A week later, the young singer was signed to a recording contract.

When Bieber's first single, "One Time," was released in May 2009, he became the biggest teenage pop star since Michael Jackson. By January 2010, the video of "One Time," posted to YouTube, had been viewed more than 100 million times. Although the song never reached number 1 on the Billboard charts, it has been downloaded illegally countless times from file-sharing websites.

Bieber's seven-song album *My World*, which contains "One Time," went platinum during its first week of release. His follow-up album, 2010's *My World 2.0*, debuted at number 1 on the album charts. This made Bieber the youngest solo singer to accomplish this feat since a young Stevie Wonder released the album *Recorded Live: The 12 Year Old Genius* in 1963.

In 2010, Bieber experienced full media saturation. He appeared on TV shows such as *Saturday Night Live*, *The Daily Show*, and *CSI: Crime Scene Investigation*. His 3-D concert film, *Justin Bieber: Never Say Never*, which features scenes from his 2010 *My World* tour, grossed $29 million the first weekend. This figure put Bieber's movie ahead of those by other pop sensations such as the Jonas Brothers' *The 3D Concert Experience* and Michael Jackson's *This Is It*. In 2012, he released the album *Believe*, and in 2013, he released the acoustic version of the album. In 2015, his album *Purpose* had three singles reach number 1 on the Billboard Hot 100. He has been the source of significant controversy since he was discovered, as much for his actions as for his music. While he has a large number of fans who call themselves "Beliebers," he has also faced ridicule for his voice and appearance. Additionally, he has been arrested several times for things such as driving under the influence (DUI), assault, and vandalism.

to her unique singing style that merged hip-hop sensibilities with soulful R&B.

When Beyoncé released her first solo album, *Dangerously in Love*, in June 2003, it entered the charts at number 1. The infectious lead single, "Crazy in Love," featuring her future husband, JAY-Z, stayed at number 1 for two months. Beyoncé's second album, *B'Day*, was released on her 25th birthday in 2006 and produced a number of hit singles, such as "Irreplaceable." Beyoncé's third studio album, *I Am … Sasha Fierce*, debuted at number 1 upon its release in 2008. The album included massive hits such as "Single Ladies (Put a Ring on It)." In 2011, Beyoncé released an album called *4*, which had a wide range of musical styles, from ballads to dance tracks reminiscent of Motown songs. In 2013, she released a visual self-titled album, which had a music video for each song. In 2016, Beyoncé released the hit album *Lemonade*, which was the best-selling album in 2016 by any artist, selling 2.5 million copies. Beyoncé has also had a successful movie career, appearing in *The Pink Panther*, *Dreamgirls*, and *Cadillac Records*. In addition, Beyoncé has her own clothing line and fragrance, and she founded the Survivor Charity, a community outreach organization. Beyoncé is one of the most powerful and popular artists in pop music, producing hits with every album she releases.

Rihanna: International Pop Superstar

So far, the 21st century has been filled with powerful female pop superstars such as Rihanna. In 2005, 17-year-old Barbados-born singer Rihanna (Robyn Rihanna Fenty) combined the island sound of reggae with dance pop and R&B on her debut single "Pon de Replay," and she quickly became an international singing sensation.

Rihanna had star qualities even as a young girl, often winning talent shows and beauty contests. She was discovered in 2005 by Evan Rogers, who was vacationing in Barbados with his wife. Rogers was an extremely successful pop producer whose roster included superstars *NSYNC, Christina Aguilera, and Jessica Simpson. Rogers offered Rihanna a chance to record, and her first two albums, *Music of the Sun* and *A Girl Like Me*, were a hit with fans. Music reviewers praised Rihanna's third album, 2007's *Good Girl Gone Bad*, which features up-tempo, soulful dance tracks and collaborators such as Justin Timberlake and Timbaland. The album sold millions of copies and generated the hit lead single "Umbrella," which featured JAY-Z.

Since then, Rihanna has collaborated on hits with rapper Eminem and released several albums, including *Rated R* in 2009 and *Loud* in 2010. By 2011, when she was 23 years old, she had 10 number 1 Billboard hits, making her the youngest artist to achieve that feat. In 2011, she released the album *Talk That Talk* with the hit "We Found Love," and in 2012,

Rihanna is only the second recording artist in history to achieve more than 30 number-1 hits in their career.

history, and she continues to be a role model for fans as well as a fierce pop superstar.

Kesha

Kesha rose to pop music stardom in 2010 with the release of her first single, "Tik Tok," off of her debut album *Animal*. The song gathered a following, which resulted in the album hitting the top of the album charts. Pop music stardom seemed to be her destiny—her mother is a songwriter whose biggest hit was for country superstar Dolly Parton. At 17, she left school to work with producer Dr. Luke and became a back-up vocalist for artists such as Britney Spears. Her big break occurred when she received a recording contract with RCA in 2009 after appearing on Flo Rida's song "Right Round."

she released *Unapologetic* with the hit song "Diamonds." In 2016, she released her eighth album, *Anti*. In July 2017, her single "Pose" off of the album made her only the second artist in history to have 30 number 1 songs—Madonna has the lead at 46. Her 2016 album has solidified her spot as one of the most successful pop stars in music

In 2010, *Animal* was released, followed by *Warrior* in 2012. In 2013, the companion album *Deconstructed* was released. However, shortly after these album successes, Kesha experienced personal troubles. Early in 2014,

AN EVER-CHANGING ART FORM 85

BOY BANDS OF THE 2000S

The Backstreet Boys, while still immensely popular, do not experience the same amount of rabid fan fascination that they used to, and *NSYNC has disbanded. In their place, other stars have risen.

The Jonas Brothers—Joe, Kevin, and Nick—released an album in 2006, but they did not start experiencing success until 2007, when they signed with Disney's Hollywood Records. They released a self-titled album, which went to number 5 on the charts, and began making regular appearances on the Disney Channel. In 2008, the group released *A Little Bit Longer*, which debuted at number 1 on the Billboard 200, and the brothers became pop superstars. In 2009, they released a concert documentary, *Jonas Brothers: The 3D Concert Experience*, and also released their new album *Lines, Vines and Trying Times*. From 2009 to 2010, they starred in the Disney Series *JONAS*, which was later changed to *JONAS L.A.* After going on hiatus and releasing their fifth album, *V.*, in 2013, they announced that the band had broken up, but both Nick and Joe have experienced continued musical success.

In 2012, the band One Direction made its debut in the United States. Made up of members Niall Horan, Zayn Malik, Liam Payne, Harry Styles, and Louis Tomlinson, the group got its start on the British TV show *The X Factor*. Although they did not win, they were offered a recording contract by Simon Cowell shortly after that season ended. Their album *Up All Night* was released in the UK in 2011 and the United States in 2012, and it went to number 1 on the Billboard album charts. Another album was released that same year in the United States, called *Take Me Home*, and in 2013, the group released the documentary *One Direction: This Is Us* and the album *Midnight Memories*. In 2014, they released the album *Four*, and during the tour, they announced that Malik had left the group. One Direction released a final album as a group in 2015, called *Made in the A.M.* In early 2016, they confirmed they were going their separate ways and are currently working on establishing solo careers.

she was treated for an eating disorder, and later in the year, she filed a lawsuit against Dr. Luke for sexual assault and sexual harassment. Meanwhile, he sued her for damaging his reputation, which is known as defamation. Kesha experienced additional heartbreak during this time—the court decision would not free her from her contract with Dr. Luke's label. However, Kesha had widespread support, not only among her fans, but among powerful performers such as Lady Gaga, Adele, and Taylor Swift. In late 2016, she went back into the studio to create a powerful, personal album called *Rainbow*. The first single, "Praying"—a liberating song with emotional and inspirational lyrics about her struggles with Dr. Luke—was released in July 2017. Kesha wrote about the song:

> *I have channeled my feelings of severe hopelessness and depression, I've overcome obstacles, and I have found strength in myself even when it felt out of reach. I've found what I had thought was an unobtainable place of peace. This song is about coming to feel empathy for someone else even if they hurt you or scare you. It's a song about learning to be proud of the person you are even during low moments when you feel alone. It's also about hoping everyone, even someone who hurt you, can heal ...*
>
> *I hope this song reaches people who are in the midst of struggles, to let them know that no matter how bad it seems now, you can get through it. If you have love and truth on your side, you will never be defeated. Don't give up on yourself.*[47]

The Fame of Mother Monster

One of the most successful and beloved pop stars was born with the name Stefani Joanne Angelina Germanotta. However, she is known in the music world as Lady Gaga, or "Mother Monster" to her fans. Not only does she create enormously popular music, she is also an ally and icon for the LGBT+ community. In addition, she goes out of her way for fans and shows her appreciation in a way few pop stars do. Lady Gaga studied music from an early age and was performing onstage by the time she was a teenager. After graduating from high school, she studied music at New York University at the Tisch School of the Arts. While she dropped out after two years, she immediately started working on her music career, writing songs for other pop artists such as Britney Spears. In 2007, she was signed to Interscope Records, and in 2008, she released her first album, *The Fame*. With this album, she immediately had the love and devotion of fans with infectious songs such as "Poker Face" and "Just Dance," both of which went to number 1 on the Billboard charts. "Paparazzi" and "LoveGame" from *The Fame* also went to number 1 on the pop charts, which made her the first artist in the history of the pop chart to have four number 1 singles from a debut album. Not only did fans love the album, critics did, too. It earned Lady Gaga five Grammy nominations and sold more than

8 million copies.

Additionally, Lady Gaga had created a character for herself in the music world, which had not truly been seen since David Bowie in his Ziggy Stardust period. Lady Gaga even modeled her character after Bowie during this period and her stage name came from a Queen song, "Radio Ga Ga." She came on the music scene with a unique fashion style, which she continued to exhibit throughout her career. Her unusual fashion choices have included an all-lace dress that covered even her face, a cage headdress, a flower headdress which encircled her head, and a meat dress which caused controversy and made headlines. Around the time of her *Joanne* album and tour, she made a pink cowboy hat a wardrobe staple.

In 2009, Lady Gaga released her follow-up album *The Fame Monster*, which was just as loved by fans and critics as her first album. It generated the hits "Bad Romance," "Telephone" (featuring Beyoncé), and "Alejandro." In 2010, just two years after she released her first album, she was one of the most successful artists in pop music. In this year, her tour for *The Fame Monster* sold out, and she was listed as one of the 100 Most Influential People by *TIME* magazine, one of the most powerful women in the world by *Forbes* magazine, and artist of the year by *Billboard* magazine.

Her third album, *Born This Way*, included hits such as "The Edge of Glory," "Judas," and the title track, which was praised for its inclusion of LGBT+ people. In 2012, Lady Gaga and her mother, Cynthia Germanotta, founded the Born This Way Foundation with the goals of creating a braver and kinder world. The foundation provides youth with opportunities, launches programs tailored to young people, and also has a focus on mental health to remove the stigma, or negative view, surrounding issues such as anxiety, depression, and post-traumatic stress disorder (PTSD). In addition, the foundation has helped thousands of LGBT+ youth and launched initiatives such as Channel Kindness, #KindMonsters, and #HackHarassment to end bullying of the LGBT+ community. She has created a safe space for her fans, which makes them appreciate her even more. Additionally, on a tour called the *Born This Way Ball*, she brought the Born Brave Bus with her, which was a spot for her fans, called "Little Monsters," to unite before the show and discuss issues such as bullying and mental health. Lady Gaga has been open about her own mental health struggles and her severe chronic pain condition fibromyalgia, which was shown in her Netflix documentary *Five Foot Two*. Her openness about these issues helps remove the negativity surrounding the conditions, which leads to more people being open to receiving treatment when they find they are also affected.

In 2013, Lady Gaga released her fourth album, *Artpop*, which did not do as well as her first

Lady Gaga is known for pushing boundaries with her songs and fashion choices, but she is also known as a genuinely talented musician.

AN EVER-CHANGING ART FORM

albums but was still a success and loved by fans. The album generated hits such as the title track and "Applause." This album was followed by *Cheek to Cheek* the next year, which she recorded with the legendary Tony Bennett. Around this time, she also started acting in notable shows and movies, such as *Sin City: A Dame to Kill For*. Her breakout roles came in *American Horror Story: Hotel* and *American Horror Story: Roanoke*. She was so loved in the show and acted so well that *American Horror Story* watchers were saddened to hear that she would not be returning for the next season. As of 2018, she still has not returned to the show. However, fans of her acting were excited to learn that she was cast to star opposite Bradley Cooper in the 2018 film *A Star Is Born*.

In October 2016, she released *Joanne* and performed a highly praised set at the 2017 Super Bowl a few months later. This is her most personal album to date and is named after her aunt, who died before Lady Gaga was born. The artwork in the album also included poems by her aunt as well as photos of her. The title track addressed her death with lyrics such as "Take my hand / Stay Joanne / Heaven's not / Ready for you / Every part of my / Aching heart / Needs you more / Than the angels do."[48] In addition, Lady Gaga also included the song "Angel Down," which was written for Trayvon Martin, a black American teenager who was shot and killed by a neighborhood watch volunteer. Martin's death sparked the Black Lives Matter movement because he had not been doing anything wrong before he was shot.

Lady Gaga has been an outspoken advocate and ally for numerous groups of people. During a candlelight vigil for the victims of the 2016 Pulse nightclub shooting in Orlando, Florida, in which 49 people were shot and killed at an LGBT+ club, Lady Gaga appeared, offering her support and an emotional speech. She urged people to love, and she expressed her unity with the community by reciting each victim's name. Lady Gaga is one of the rare influential pop music artists who does not merely say she is aligned with a cause—she goes out and offers her support in any way she can, showing the importance of being an ally and ensuring her position as a positive role model for fans. In late 2017, she announced the next step in her legacy as a pop superstar—a Las Vegas residency. Starting in late 2018, she began a 75-show residency spread over 2 years at the MGM Park Theater, joining the ranks of other legacy pop artists, such as the

Backstreet Boys, who have experienced successful Las Vegas residency shows.

Future Pop

Pop music was originally considered to be a shallow genre with simple songs. However, as the genre has evolved, so has pop music's complexity. Pop music artists are not only speaking about social issues in their music, they are also taking extra steps and showing their support for causes by creating foundations to help others, marching in protest along with average people, and speaking out at events to be there for people who are hurting.

Additionally, international styles of pop music as well as the artists who create them are finding widespread appeal throughout the world, particularly due to social media. One of these international styles, called K-pop because of its South Korean roots, draws inspiration from numerous other genres, such as hip-hop, dance, and classical.

With such a rich history of complex, influential songs, pop music seems poised to continue to evolve in exciting ways.

Notes

Introduction: Pop Music Through the Ages

1. The Editors of *Enyclopaedia Britannica*, "Popular Music," *Encylopaedia Britannica*, accessed on March 2, 2018. www.britannica.com/art/popular-music.
2. Katherine Myers, "The History of Pop Music in 5 Defining Decades," Culture Trip, July 19, 2016. theculturetrip.com/north-america/usa/california/articles/the-history-of-pop-music-in-5-defining-decades/.
3. Quoted in Jeff Nilsson, "Sexy, Simply, Sad: How Mitch Miller Defined Pop Music in the 1950s," *Saturday Evening Post*, August 4, 2010.
4. Myers, "The History of Pop Music in 5 Defining Decades."

Chapter One: "All Shook Up": Early Pop Music

5. Josh Sanburn, "All-Time 100 Songs: 'Over the Rainbow,'" *TIME*, October 21, 2011. entertain-ment.time.com/2011/10/24/the-all-time-100-songs/slide/over-the-rainbow-judy-garland/.
6. Fraser McAlpine, "Over the Rainbow: How this Powerful Song has Soundtracked History," BBC, June 6, 2017. www.bbc.co.uk/music/articles/efc32112-f7a0-49b3-bfae-6e6a72a80572.
7. Fred Bronson, *The Billboard Book of Number One Hits*. New York, NY: Billboard Books, 1997, p. xxiii.
8. Quoted in Peter Guralnick, "Elvis Presley: How Sun Records Boss Sam Phillips Discovered a Star in 1954," *Independent*, October 30, 2015. www.independent.co.uk/arts-entertainment/music/features/elvis-presley-how-sun-records-boss-sam-phillips-discovered-a-star-in-1954-a6713891.html.

9. Quoted in Joel Williamson, *Elvis Presley: A Southern Life*. New York, NY: Oxford University Press, 2015, "Sam's First Elvis Record."
10. Quoted in David Brackett, ed., *The Pop, Rock, and Soul Reader*. New York, NY: Oxford Univer-sity Press, 2005, p. 94.
11. "Music: Teeners' Hero," *TIME*, May 14, 1956. content.time.com/time/magazine/article/0,9171,808428,00.html.
12. Quoted in Elizabeth Kaye, "Sam Phillips: The Rolling Stone Interview," *Rolling Stone*, February 13, 1986. www.rollingstone.com/music/features/the-rolling-stone-interview-sam-phillips-19860213.
13. Robert Palmer, *Blues & Chaos: The Music Writing of Robert Palmer*. New York, NY: Scribner, 2009, p. 107.
14. Quoted in June Bundy, "Vox Jox," *Billboard*, December 15, 1958, p. 8.

Chapter Two:
Surfing Songs and Strawberry Fields

15. "Surfin USA," track 1 on the Beach Boys, *Surfin' USA*. Capitol, 1963.
16. Jordan Runtagh, "Beach Boys' 'Pet Sounds': 15 Things You Didn't Know," *Rolling Stone*, May 16, 2016. www.rollingstone.com/music/news/beach-boys-pet-sounds-15-things-you-didnt-know-20160516.
17. Jason Guriel, "How Pet Sounds Invented the Modern Pop Album," *The Atlantic*, May 16, 2016. www.theatlantic.com/entertainment/archive/2016/05/how-pet-sounds-invented-the-modern-pop-album/482940/.
18. Quoted in Runtagh, "Beach Boys' 'Pet Sounds': 15 Things You Didn't Know."
19. Runtagh, "Beach Boys' 'Pet Sounds': 15 Things You Didn't Know."
20. Quoted in Keith Badman, *The Beatles: Off the Record*. London, UK: Omnibus Press, 2009, "Thursday, 24 November."
21. Quoted in Todd Van Luling, "The Beach Boys Finally Confirm Those Legends About 'Pet Sounds,'" *Huffington Post*, May 16, 2016. www.huffingtonpost.com/entry/beach-boys-pet-sounds_us_5730fcd5e4b096e9f09258e4.
22. Quoted in Luling, "The Beach Boys Finally Confirm Those Legends About 'Pet Sounds.'"

23. Michael S. Rosenwald, "Charles Manson's Surreal Summer with the Beach Boys," *Washington Post*, November 20, 2017. www.washingtonpost.com/news/retropolis/wp/2017/11/20/charles-mansons-surreal-summer-with-the-beach-boys-group-sex-dumpster-diving-and-rock-n-roll/?utm_term=.5b1ab9219ae6.
24. "The Beatles Bio," *Rolling Stone*, accessed on March 11, 2018. www.rollingstone.com/music/artists/the-beatles/biography.
25. "She Loves You," track 4 on the Beatles, *The Beatles/1962–1966*. EMI Records, 1973.
26. Quoted in Chris Smith, *101 Albums That Changed Popular Music*. New York, NY: Oxford University Press, 2009, p. 46.
27. Larry Starr and Christopher Waterman, *American Popular Music from Minstrelsy to MTV*. New York, NY: Oxford University Press, 2003, pp. 293–294.

Chapter Three:
The Rise of Pop Icons

28. "The Jackson 5," Biography.com, accessed on March 12, 2018. www.biography.com/people/groups/the-jackson-5.
29. "Bee Gees Bio," *Rolling Stone*, accessed on March 12, 2018. www.allmusic.com/artist/bee-gees-mn0000043714/biography.
30. "ABBA," Rock & Roll Hall of Fame, accessed on March 12, 2018. www.rockhall.com/inductees/abba.
31. Chloe Kerr, "Thank You for the Music," *The Sun*, December 18, 2017. www.thesun.co.uk/tvandshowbiz/2059774/abba-greatest-hits-split-reunion-benny-andersson-bjorn-agnetha/.
32. "ABBA," Rock & Roll Hall of Fame.
33. Quoted in Michael Shore, *The Rolling Stone Book of Rock Video*. New York, NY: Quill, 1984, p. 15.
34. Tom McGrath, "Integrating MTV" in *Rock and Roll is Here to Stay*, ed. William McKeen. New York, NY: W. W. Norton & Company, 2000, p. 461.
35. Quoted in Alicia Adamczyk, "Michael Jackson's 'Thriller' Just Smashed Another Record," *TIME*, December 16, 2015. time.com/money/4151215/michael-jacksons-thriller-album-sales-record/.
36. Quoted in Lucy O'Brien, *Madonna: Like an Icon*. New York, NY: Harper-Entertainment, 2007, p. 71.

Chapter Four:
Tearin' Up Fans' Hearts: Teen Pop of the 1990s

37. Stephen Kijak, dir. *Backstreet Boys: Show 'Em What You're Made Of.* Brooklyn, NY: FilmRise, 2015.
38. Quoted in Nolan Feeney, "The Oral History of the Backstreet Boys, as Told by the Backstreet Boys," *Entertainment Weekly*, February 22, 2017. ew.com/music/2017/02/22/backstreet-boys-oral-history/.
39. Kijak, dir. *Backstreet Boys: Show 'Em What You're Made Of.*
40. "I Want It That Way," track 2 on Backstreet Boys, *Millennium*. Jive, 1999.
41. Kijak, dir. *Backstreet Boys: Show 'Em What You're Made Of.*
42. Kijak, dir. *Backstreet Boys: Show 'Em What You're Made Of.*
43. Kijak, dir. *Backstreet Boys: Show 'Em What You're Made Of.*

Chapter Five:
An Ever-Changing Art Form

44. Ryan Dombal, "Justin Timberlake: *The 20/20 Experience*," Pitchfork, March 19, 2013. pitchfork.com/reviews/albums/17736-justin-timberlake-the-2020-experience.
45. Jamieson Cox, "Justin Timberlake: *Man of the Woods*," Pitchfork, February 2, 2018. pitchfork.com/reviews/albums/justin-timberlake-man-of-the-woods/.
46. Jasmine Grant, "The Justin Timberlake Backlash Isn't New—But Here's Why Everyone's Talking About It Now," *Bustle*, February 2018. www.billboard.com/articles/columns/chart-beat/8099090/justin-timberlake-earns-fourth-no-1-album-on-billboard-200-chart.
47. Kesha, "Kesha Fights Back in Her New Single, 'Praying,'" Lenny Letter, July 6, 2017. www.lennyletter.com/story/kesha-fights-back-in-her-new-single-praying.
48. "Joanne," track 3 on Lady Gaga, *Joanne*. Interscope Records, 2016.

ESSENTIAL ALBUMS

Publisher's note: Some albums may contain strong language or explicit content.

Backstreet Boys
Backstreet Boys (1997)
In a World Like This (2013)
Millennium (1999)

Beach Boys
Pet Sounds (1966)
Surfer Girl (1963)

The Beatles
Abbey Road (1969)
Meet the Beatles (1964)
Sgt. Pepper's Lonely Hearts Club Band (1967)

Beyoncé
Dangerously in Love (2003)
Lemonade (2016)

Britney Spears
… Baby One More Time (1999)
Oops! … I Did It Again (2000)

Elvis Presley
Elvis Presley (1956)

Fleetwood Mac
Rumours (1977)

Janet Jackson
Control (1986)

Justin Timberlake
FutureSex/LoveSounds (2006)
The 20/20 Experience (2013)

Kesha
Rainbow (2017)

Lady Gaga
Born This Way (2011)
The Fame (2008)
The Fame Monster (2009)

Michael Jackson
Off the Wall (1979)
Thriller (1982)

Madonna
Like a Virgin (1984)
Ray of Light (1998)

*NSYNC
No Strings Attached (2000)

Spice Girls
Spice (1996)
Spiceworld (1997)

POP MUSIC: CHART-TOPPERS THROUGHOUT HISTORY

For More Information

Books

Roberts, Jeremy. *The Beatles: Music Revolutionaries*. Minneapolis, MN: Lerner, 2011.
   This book tells the story of one of the most commercially successful and critically acclaimed acts in the history of popular music. It covers the Beatles' journey from Liverpool, England, to the world stage while working in genres ranging from folk rock to psychedelic pop.

Seabrook, John. *The Song Machine: Inside the Hit Factory*. New York, NY: W. W. Norton & Company, 2015.
   Seabrook's book is a fascinating read that traces the stories behind addictive pop songs by artists such as Britney Spears and Katy Perry, as well as the producers who help create these catchy songs.

Smith, Chris. *101 Albums That Changed Popular Music*. New York, NY: Oxford University Press, 2009.
   This book covers a wide range of albums that influenced pop music from the early 1950s to the 1990s.

Spitz, Bob. *The Beatles: The Biography*. New York, NY: Little, Brown and Company, 2005.
   This extensive biography of the Beatles is a must-read for fans of the group and those interested in the complex history of the band.

Stanley, Bob. *Yeah! Yeah! Yeah! The Story of Pop Music from Bill Haley to Beyoncé*. New York, NY: W. W. Norton & Company, 2014.
   This detailed book explores the history of pop music, telling behind-the-scenes stories about the creation of the Beach Boys, the Beatles, ABBA, Michael Jackson, and more.

Websites

AllMusic
www.allmusic.com
> The AllMusic website is one of the most comprehensive music guides on the internet. The website has in-depth information about various kinds of music, especially pop music, and information on new releases.

Billboard
www.billboard.com
> *Billboard* magazine's website features music, news, reviews, and the latest songs and albums and where they are on the charts.

Born This Way Foundation
bornthisway.foundation
> Lady Gaga's foundation has helped thousands of young adults and has information on mental wellness and current campaigns.

Rolling Stone
www.rollingstone.com
> *Rolling Stone* has been covering pop stars and the music industry since the 1960s. The magazine's website contains the latest music and pop culture news, biographies of numerous pop stars, and music, movie, and video reviews.

Index

A

ABBA, 44, 48, 51–53
ABBAWORLD, 52
Abbey Road (The Beatles), 46
Across the Universe (film), 44
Aguilera, Christina, 10, 73, 75, 79, 84
A Hard Day's Night (film), 44
"A Hard Day's Night" (The Beatles), 42
Artpop (Lady Gaga), 89

B

… Baby One More Time (Spears), 73
backlash, 6, 24, 51, 59, 78, 80–81
Backstreet Boys, 9, 61–74, 77–78, 86, 90
Backstreet Boys: Show 'Em What You're Made Of (documentary), 66, 69
Beach Boys, The, 29–34, 36, 38
Beatlemania, 9, 40–41, 44, 66
Beatles, The, 9, 24, 29, 33, 35, 37, 41–49, 53, 61, 64, 71, 78, 91
Bee Gees, 48, 50–51
Berlin, Irving, 11–13
Beyoncé, 11, 75, 81–84, 88
Bieber, Justin, 83
Bill Haley and His Comets, 11, 20
"Billie Jean" (Jackson), 54

Black and Blue (Backstreet Boys), 68
Born This Way Foundation, 88
Born This Way (Lady Gaga), 88
boy bands, 9, 61–66, 69–71, 77, 86
Brill Building, 38–41
Britney Jean (Spears), 75

C

Carter, Nick, 65
Celebrity (*NSYNC), 73
Columbia Records, 7, 18, 52
conspiracy theories, 24–25, 76
Control (Jackson), 57

D

Dorough, Howie, 65

E

Ed Sullivan Show, The, 24, 41–42
Epstein, Brian, 41
"Everybody (Backstreet's Back)" (Backstreet Boys), 67, 71

F

Fame, The (Lady Gaga), 67, 88
Fame Monster, The (Lady Gaga), 88
Femme Fatale (Spears), 75

Fisher, Eddie, 17, 19
Fleetwood Mac, 50
Frankie Valli and the Four Seasons, 44
Full House (TV show), 38
FutureSex/LoveSounds (Timberlake), 79

G

Garland, Judy, 15–16
Gershwin, George, 11, 13
Glory (Spears), 75
Goffin, Gerry, 38–39

H

Hammerstein, Oscar, II, 11
Harrison, George, 41, 44–45, 47
Help! (film), 44
"Helter Skelter" (The Beatles), 35, 37
Holland-Dozier-Holland, 40
Holly, Buddy, 11, 26–28, 41

I

"I'll Be Loving You (Forever)" (New Kids on the Block), 61
"I'll Never Break Your Heart" (Backstreet Boys), 67
In a World Like This (Backstreet Boys), 69
In the Zone (Spears), 75
"I Want It That Way" (Backstreet Boys), 67
"I Want To Hold Your Hand" (The Beatles), 41–42
"I Want You Back" (Jackson 5), 48
"I Want You Back" (*NSYNC), 72

J

Jackson, Janet, 57–59, 78
Jackson, Michael, 9, 48, 50, 54–55, 57, 59, 61, 67, 83, 91
Jacksons, The, 9, 48–50, 61
Janet Jackson's Rhythm Nation 1814 (Jackson), 57
Jardine, Al, 29–30, 38
Jersey Boys, 44–45
Joanne (Lady Gaga), 58, 90
Johnston, Bruce, 29, 31, 33, 38
Jonas Brothers, 9, 83, 86
Justified (Timberlake), 78

K

Kesha, 6–7, 78, 85–87
King, Carole, 38–39
"Kokomo" (Beach Boys), 38

L

Lady Gaga, 11, 77–78, 86–91
"Larger Than Life" (Backstreet Boys), 68
Las Vegas, Nevada, 70, 90
Lavigne, Avril, 75–76
Lennon, John, 41, 43–44, 46–47
Lewis, Jerry Lee, 22, 25–26, 28
LGBT+ community, 16, 87–88, 90
Like a Virgin (Madonna), 60
Littrell, Brian, 65
Love, Mike, 29–30, 38

M

Madonna, 48, 59–61, 76, 85
"Mamma Mia" (ABBA), 52
Mamma Mia! (film and musical), 44, 52, 58

Man of the Woods (Timberlake), 6, 58, 78, 80–81
Manson, Charles, 34–37
Marks, David, 29–30, 38
"Material Girl" (Madonna), 60
McCartney, Paul, 9, 33, 37, 41, 44–45, 54
McLean, A. J., 65, 71
#MeToo, 6, 81
Millennium (Backstreet Boys), 67–68, 74
Miller, Mitch, 7, 17
MTV, 53–54, 57, 60, 74

N

Neptunes, 78, 81
Never Gone (Backstreet Boys), 69
New Kids on the Block, 9, 61–65, 69–70
NKOTBSB (New Kids on the Block and Backstreet Boys), 62
No Strings Attached (*NSYNC), 72–73
*NSYNC, 9, 63, 70–74, 77–80, 84, 86

O

Off the Wall (Jackson), 54, 60
One Direction, 9, 63, 86
Oops! … I Did It Again (Spears), 74
"Over the Rainbow," 15–17

P

Pearlman, Lou, 65, 70–72
Pet Sounds (Beach Boys), 31–33, 36
"Praying" (Kesha), 6–7, 87

Presley, Elvis, 6–8, 11, 20–25, 28, 41, 44, 76, 78, 91
Price, Vincent, 55

Q

"Quit Playing Games (With My Heart)" (Backstreet Boys), 67

R

Rainbow (Kesha), 87
Ray of Light (Madonna), 61
Recording Industry Association of America (RIAA), 26, 52, 54, 67
Richardson, Kevin, 65, 71
Rihanna, 75, 84–85
Robinson, Smokey, 40

S

"Say You'll Be There" (Spice Girls), 64
Sgt. Pepper's Lonely Hearts Club Band (The Beatles), 33, 44–47
"Shape of My Heart" (Backstreet Boys), 68
sheet music, 13–15
Spears, Britney, 10, 73–75, 77, 85, 87
Spice Girls, 9–10, 64–65, 67
Spice (Spice Girls), 64
"Spice Up Your Life" (Spice Girls), 9, 64
Spiceworld (Spice Girls), 64
Spice World: The Movie, 64
Starr, Ringo, 41, 44, 46
"Strawberry Fields Forever" (The Beatles), 43–44
Super Bowl, 57–59, 80, 90

"Super Trouper" (ABBA), 52
Supremes, The, 40
Surfer Girl (The Beach Boys), 30
Surfin' USA (The Beach Boys), 30
synthesizer, 59–60

T
"That's All Right (Mama)" (Elvis), 22
This Is Us (Backstreet Boys), 69
Thriller (Jackson), 54–55
"Ticket to Ride" (The Beatles), 42
Timbaland, 61, 78, 81, 84
Timberlake, Justin, 6, 9, 11, 57–59, 61, 71, 73–75, 77–81, 84
TIME magazine, 15, 24, 88
Tin Pan Alley, 11, 13–15, 38, 78, 91
Total Request Live (*TRL*), 74
20/20 Experience, The (Timberlake), 79–80

U
Unbreakable (Backstreet Boys), 69
Unbreakable (Jackson), 58

W
Wallerstein, Ed, 18
"Wannabe" (Spice Girls), 64, 67
"We Can Work It Out" (The Beatles), 42
"We've Got It Goin' On" (Backstreet Boys), 65
Wilson, Brian, 29–31, 33, 38
Wilson, Carl, 29–30, 38
Wilson, Dennis, 29–30, 34–37

Y
"You Got It (The Right Stuff)" (New Kids on the Block), 61

Picture Credits

Cover (main) Aaron Amat/Shutterstock.com; cover (background), back cover, pp. 3–4, 6, 11, 29, 48, 64, 78, 92, 96–97, 99, 103–104 hxdyl/Shutterstock.com; p. 7 Kevin Winter/Getty Images for NARAS; p. 8 Popperfoto/Getty Images; p. 10 Featureflash Photo Agency/Shutterstock.com; p. 12 Bettmann/Bettmann/Getty Images; pp. 14, 19, 21 Hulton Archive/Getty Images; p. 16 Metro-Goldwyn-Mayer/Getty Images; p. 18 Blank Archives/Getty Images; p. 23 Charles Trainor/The LIFE Images Collection/Getty Images; p. 25 ROBERTO SCHMIDT/AFP/Getty Images; p. 27 John Rodgers/Redferns/Getty Images; p. 30 Michael Ochs Archive/Getty Images; p. 32 RB/Redferns/Getty Images; p. 35 Sahm Doherty/The LIFE Images Collection/Getty Images; p. 36 Kyle Gustafson/For The Washington Post via Getty Images; pp. 39, 49, 53 Michael Ochs Archives/Getty Images; p. 42 Tracksimages.com/Alamy Stock Photo; p. 45 John Stillwell/PA Images via Getty Images; p. 47 Ben185/iStock/Thinkstock; p. 56 MCA/Universal/Courtesy: Everett Collection; p. 58 Harry Langdon/Getty Images; p. 60 Tony Barson/WireImage/Getty Images; p. 62 Kevin Winter/DMI/The LIFE Picture Collection/Getty Images; pp. 66, 69 Brill/ullstein bild via Getty Images; p. 68 Jim Steinfeldt/Michael Ochs Archives/Getty Images; p. 72 KMazur/WireImage/Getty Images; pp. 74, 82, 85 Kevin Mazur/WireImage/Getty Images; p. 75 Mick Hutson/Redferns/Getty Images; p. 80 Dave J Hogan/Dave J Hogan/Getty Images; p. 89 Gary Miller/Getty Images.

About
the Author

Nicole Horning has written a number of books for young adults. She holds a bachelor's degree in English and a master's degree in special education from D'Youville College in Buffalo, New York. She lives in Western New York with her cats, Khaleesi and Evie, and reads and writes in her free time.